Why Don't Sharks Have BONES?

This edition published in 2021 by Arcturus Publishing Limited
26/27 Bickels Yard, 151-153 Bermondsey Street,
London SE1 3HA

Copyright © Arcturus Holdings Limited

All rights reserved. No part of this publication may be reproduced, stored in a retrieval system, or transmitted, in any form or by any means, electronic, mechanical, photocopying, recording, or otherwise, without prior written permission in accordance with the provisions of the Copyright Act 1956 (as amended). Any person or persons who do any unauthorized act in relation to this publication may be liable to criminal prosecution and civil claims for damages.

Illustrator: Luke Séguin-Magee
Authors: Clare Hibbert, William Potter, and Marc Powell
Editors: Susie Rae and Joe Harris
Designer: Rosie Bellwood

CH007051NT
Supplier: 10, Date 0621, Print run 11572

Printed in the UK

CONTENTS

COOL CETACEANS 5

SUPER SHARKS 27

DEEPLY DIPPY 59

DARKEST DEPTHS 89

SOMETHING'S FISHY 101

ARE YOU READY TO MAKE A SPLASH?

Then zip up your wet suit and strap on your scuba tank for a deep dive into the wet and wonderful world of undersea creatures.

You'll meet the biggest creature that ever lived on our planet, speedy sharks, venomous jellyfish, exploding crustaceans, the fierce, fanged monsters that live miles down in the dark depths, and much, much more!

COOL CETACEANS

WHAT'S A CETACEAN?

Cetaceans are aquatic mammals that include toothed whales—such as sperm whales, orcas, narwhals, and dolphins—and baleen whales, like the blue whale, right whale, and bowhead.

DID YOU KNOW?

The arteries of the massive blue whale are so huge that a human baby could crawl through them.

WHAT IS THE LARGEST ANIMAL IN THE WORLD...EVER?

The blue whale is the largest creature known to have lived on our planet—bigger than any dinosaur. The longest blue whale ever found measured just over 33m (110ft). That's the length of nine family cars end to end!

HOW HEAVY IS A BLUE WHALE?

A blue whale can weigh up to 125 metric tons (250,000lbs). That's as much as 23 elephants, 230 cows, or 1,800 adult men.

HOW HEAVY IS A BLUE WHALE'S TONGUE?

A blue whale's tongue can weigh the same as an elephant.

DID YOU KNOW?

A baby blue whale drinks 0.28 metric tons (60 gallons) of milk from its mother every day.

HOW FAST DOES A BLUE WHALE'S HEART BEAT?

The heart of a blue whale only beats eight to ten times a minute. (A human heart averages around 75 beats per minute.)

HOW DOES A WHALE SEE WHAT'S BEHIND IT?

Whales can't actually move their eyeballs. In order to see behind, a whale has to move its entire body.

HOW DEEP DO WHALES DIVE?

A sperm whale can dive to depths of 2km (1.25 miles).

WHY ARE WHALES SO CRUSTY?

Because whales are so slow-moving, barnacles often get attached to them. They can comfortably carry up to 454kg (1,000lb) of barnacles around with them!

HOW FAR DOES A WHALE NOISE TRAVEL?

Using sonar equipment, scientists can detect the sounds made by fin whales and blue whales from up to 850km (528 miles) away.

HOW DO YOU MAKE A SHARK EXPLODE?

Killer whales have been known to attack sharks by launching themselves into their prey's stomach like a torpedo. The force of the impact can cause the shark to explode.

ARE SOME WHALES TOOTHLESS?

Yes. Whales without teeth are called baleen whales. Blue whales, humpback whales, right whales, and gray (sometimes spelled grey) whales are all baleen whales. They have bristly baleen instead of teeth, which they use to "'sieve" food from the water.

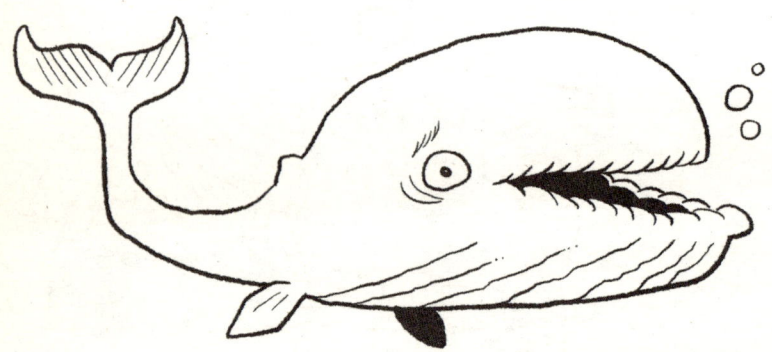

WHY DO WHALES GET TRAPPED ON BEACHES?

Whales sometimes beach themselves (get stranded on land) and are unable to swim back into the sea. If a whale is stranded, its distress call brings other whales to help, which sometimes leads to whole schools of whales being beached at the same time.

ARE DOLPHINS WHALES?

Yes. The two main types of whale are whales with teeth and whales without teeth. Dolphins are toothed whales. Other toothed whales include sperm whales and belugas. Orcas, also known as killer whales, are a type of dolphin.

HOW MANY TYPES OF DOLPHIN ARE THERE?

Experts cannot agree on an exact figure, but there are about 40. One problem is that not everyone agrees on which species are dolphins. Another is that some kinds are rare and are dying out.

WHAT ARE PORPOISES?

Porpoises are the smallest members of the whale family. They are only 1.5-2.5m (5-8ft) long. The harbor (or harbour) porpoise is the best known. It is found in cool, coastal waters all over the northern hemisphere.

DID YOU KNOW?

If a dolphin loses its tail, scientists can attach an artificial rubber tail made from the same material used to make Formula 1 car tires. It's proven to work as well as the real thing!

WHICH ANIMALS EAT DOLPHINS?

Sharks eat dolphins. Many dolphins have shark-bite scars on their bodies, so at least some of them get away. Orcas eat dolphins too—even though they belong to the same family.

HOW MANY TEETH DO DOLPHINS HAVE?

Dolphins have wide, cone-shaped teeth, just right for grasping slippery prey. One set of between 60 and 100 teeth lasts them a lifetime. The teeth start coming through when baby dolphins are about five weeks old.

HOW DO DOLPHINS FIND FOOD?

Dolphins make high-pitched clicks that travel through the water. The clicking sounds bounce off objects, sending echoes back to the dolphins. This is called echolocation. As they receive the echoes of the clicks, dolphins can build a detailed picture of what is in the water. They can tell the exact shape and structure of things and how far away they are.

DOES A DOLPHIN HAVE A MELON IN ITS HEAD?

A dolphin's bulging forehead is a vital part of its echolocation equipment. The bulge is a fatty organ called the "melon." Its job is to precisely direct or point the dolphin's clicks so that picture it builds is as accurate as possible.

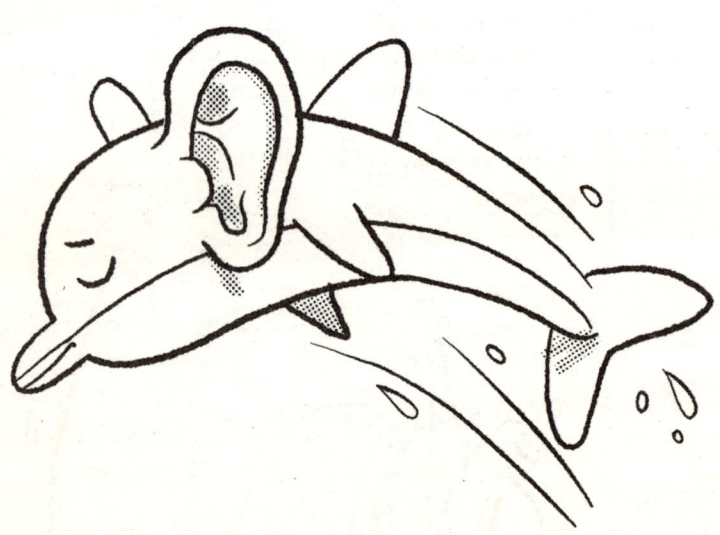

DO DOLPHINS HAVE EARS?

Dolphins have internal ears. Some sounds reach dolphin ears through small openings just behind each eye. Most sounds, however, reach their ears by vibrating, or wobbling, along their lower jaws.

HOW DO DOLPHINS SLEEP?

Dolphins sleep with one eye open! They shut down each side of their brain separately to rest.

DID YOU KNOW?

Fishing nets are designed with holes in the bottom to let dolphins and other big creatures escape. The nets work because fish, such as haddock, are not brainy enough to realize they can swim downward!

DO DOLPHINS CRY?

Yes, dolphins' eyes "weep" all the time. The oily tears keep their eyes clean—they're not a sign that dolphins feel sad!

ARE DOLPHINS FUSSY EATERS?

Dolphins have taste buds at the base of their tongue. Experts are still investigating dolphins' sense of taste, and we do not know very much about it. However, dolphins appear to prefer certain foods to others.

WHAT'S A BAIT BALL?

Dolphins have some cunning hunting methods. They often team up to drive fish into a ball shape called a bait ball. Other tricks include whacking fish with their tails to stun them or herding fish into the shallows.

ARE DOLPHINS BIRDWATCHERS?

Dolphins often poke their heads above the surface to look around. This is called spy-hopping. They look out for big crowds of seabirds—a clue that there'll be plenty of fish in the water below.

DID YOU KNOW?

Atlantic white-sided dolphins like company so much that they have been spotted in groups of up to 1,000.

HOW FRIENDLY ARE DOLPHINS?

Dolphins are very sociable and live in groups called pods. They touch each other when they are being friendly. They pat, stroke, and nuzzle their friends with their flippers and snouts.

CAN DOLPHINS SMELL?

Dolphins have no olfactory (smelling) nerves, so they cannot smell at all. However, they can detect chemicals in the water using their taste buds.

CAN FLIPPERS BE USED LIKE HANDS?

Dolphins have extra touch receptors on their flippers, so these are more sensitive than other parts of their bodies. Dolphins sometimes use their flippers to feel for crustaceans hidden in the sand of the seabed.

CAN DOLPHINS USE A MIRROR?

Dolphins can recognize their own reflections in a mirror. Only a few other animals—including humans, chimpanzees, and magpies—can do this.

CAN DOLPHINS TALK?

Dolphins make all sorts of sounds when they are "talking" to each other—squawks, whistles, squeaks, barks, groans, and moans. Experts have even noticed that each dolphin group or pod has its own way of talking, like a "dialect."

CAN WE TALK WITH DOLPHINS?

Humans are the only animals that use spoken language. However, researchers have shown that dolphins can be taught to understand sound-based language and sign language. They can even grasp how changing the order of words changes their meaning.

HOW ELSE CAN DOLPHINS COMMUNICATE?

Dolphins use body language to communicate too. A dolphin might roll over and "play dead" to show that it is no threat to another dolphin. Or it may shake its head rapidly from side to side as a sign of aggression.

DO DOLPHINS HAVE NAMES?

Dolphins often "call out" the signature whistles of other dolphins. They are using the sounds like names to call their friends!

CAN DOLPHINS SMILE?

One reason why people find dolphins so appealing may be their "smile." It's not a real smile, though—it's just the way dolphins' mouths are structured.

DO ALL DOLPHINS LIVE IN GROUPS?

It's unusual for dolphins to live alone. Sometimes lone dolphins show up near shores and choose to live near humans. It may be that they've become separated from their pod, or they are too old to keep up.

WHAT IS A POD?

Different dolphin species group together in different kinds of pods. Bottlenose dolphins often form groups of only females, or only females and calves. Dusky dolphins and white-beaked dolphins prefer to live in mixed pods that contain males, females, and calves.

DO DOLPHINS LOOK AFTER THEIR INJURED?

Dolphins have been seen staying with ill or injured members of their pod and saving their lives by nudging them up to the surface to breathe.

DO DOLPHINS EVER FIGHT EACH OTHER?

Yes. They're not always friendly! Male dolphins will fight rivals to win a mate—they fight by bashing each other with their tails.

ARE DOLPHINS CAMOUFLAGED?

Dolphins have a special kind of camouflage that makes them perfectly adapted to their watery habitat. Viewed from above, their darker backs are hard to spot against the watery depths. Viewed from below, their paler undersides blend in with the sunlit surface.

HOW FAST CAN DOLPHINS SWIM?

Dolphins cruise along at 11-12km/h (7-8mph), but speed up to chase prey. Orcas can swim at 48km/h (30mph) in short bursts.

HOW FAR DO DOLPHINS SWIM?

Dolphins stick to their home ranges. Ocean species that live far away from the shore have the largest ranges, because their food is more spread out. For example, dusky dolphins range over 1,500 square km (580 square miles).

DO DOLPHINS MIGRATE?

Not really, though they might move into slightly warmer waters as the seasons change. They don't make regular long journeys like some of their whale cousins do.

DO DOLPHINS LIVE IN RIVERS?

Several kinds of dolphin live in rivers. South America's great Amazon River is home to two types—tucuxi and botos. Many river dolphins are endangered. The Yangtze river dolphin recently became extinct because of pollution.

WHAT ARE BLOWHOLES USED FOR?

Dolphins come up to the surface to breathe. They take in air and get rid of waste gas through their blowhole, a hole on the top of their head. When dolphins are underwater, a flap covers the blowhole so water can't get in. Dolphins and other toothed whales have one blowhole. The prize for the most impressive blowhole goes to the blue whale. Its blowhole sprays the water sitting on top of it up to 12m (40ft) high.

HOW LONG CAN DOLPHINS STAY UNDERWATER?

It depends on the species and their age (older dolphins have bigger lungs). The longest is about 15 minutes. Dolphins slow down their heartbeat during a dive to reduce how much oxygen they use up.

HOW MANY YOUNG DO DOLPHINS HAVE?

Most dolphin mothers give birth to a single calf—twins are very rare. The calf is born tail first and can swim right away. Its mother nudges it toward the surface to take its very first breath.

DO DOLPHINS HAVE BABYSITTERS?

Any adult in the dolphin pod will care for or discipline the calves. Female "aunts" babysit while the mothers hunt. Youngsters that don't come when they're called or misbehave in some other way are scolded with a tail slap.

HOW LONG DO DOLPHIN CALVES STAY WITH THEIR MOTHER?

Calves stick with their mamas for at least two to three years, and sometimes for as long as six years.

ARE OCEAN DOLPHINS ENDANGERED?

Unfortunately, some human activities harm dolphins. Dolphins can get trapped in large fishing nets. Many, including the rare humpback dolphin, are threatened because of pollution, which damages their habitat and the fish they eat.

SUPER SHARKS

HOW BIG DO GREAT WHITE SHARKS GET?

Great white sharks can grow up to 6.1m (20ft) long. Females are, on average, about 1m (3ft) longer than males.

DID YOU KNOW?

Great white sharks have a bite three times more powerful than that of an African lion.

WHY SHOULD YOU NEVER FLIP A SHARK?

If a shark gets turned on to its back, it goes into a state of paralysis for up to 15 minutes.

WHY DO SHARKS HAVE TO KEEP SWIMMING?

Some breeds of shark will drown if they stop swimming. They have to keep water moving through their gills at all times, so they can never really sleep.

WHAT IS THE MOST COMMON SHARK?

There are over 500 species, or types, of shark. Sharks come in many shapes and sizes. Dogfish are the most common ones. They are about 1m (3ft) long.

DO SHARKS SLEEP?

Sharks never fall deeply asleep like humans. They keep swimming to move water through their gills. They have "resting times," though, when they let one half of their brain turn off.

WHERE DO SHARKS LIVE?

Sharks live in all the world's oceans, from icy polar waters to warm, tropical seas. They also live at all levels of the ocean, from the shallows to the deep.

DO SHARKS LIVE IN RIVERS?

Bull sharks swim far up rivers and into lakes, so they are more likely to meet (and eat) bathers and swimmers than sharks that stay out at sea. Bull sharks are widespread and found in the Amazon, Zambezi, and Ganges Rivers.

HOW MANY TEETH DO SHARKS HAVE?

Sharks' teeth are replaced every couple of weeks, so they are always in peak condition. They are arranged in rows in the mouth. As one tooth or row of teeth falls out, new ones move forward to take their place. Over their lifetime, sharks may go through 20,000 teeth!

ARE ALL SHARK TEETH THE SAME?

Shark teeth come in different shapes, to suit their owners' diets. Spear-like teeth are good for catching slippery fish and squid, while blunt teeth can crush shells. Great whites have triangular cutting teeth for slicing into seals.

WHICH SHARK HAS THE BIGGEST JAW?

The great white has the largest jaw span. Its bite exerts 15 times more pressure than a human bite can.

IS THERE REALLY A COOKIECUTTER SHARK?

Yes. The cookiecutter shark is named for its unusual feeding method. It bites circular chunks out of larger animals, such as dolphins and whales. The wounds eventually heal, leaving the victims with 5-cm (2-in) round scars.

HOW DO SHARKS BREATHE?

Like all fish, sharks take in oxygen from the water. As a shark swims, it gulps in seawater and pushes it out through gill slits on the sides of its head. Inside the gills, oxygen passes from the water into the shark's bloodstream.

DID YOU KNOW?

Sharks will eat anything, even parts of their own bodies that have been bitten after an attack by another animal.

HOW FAST CAN A SHARK SWIM?

Sharks can produce short bursts of speed to catch prey—as fast as 70km/h (43mph.)

HOW MUCH FOOD DOES A SHARK EAT?

Sharks need to eat around three percent of their body weight in food each day just to survive.

DID YOU KNOW?

Little is known about the megamouth shark as it was first discovered by scientists in 1976. Only three photographs of it in its natural habitat exist in the entire world.

DO SHARKS HAVE TASTE BUDS?

Sharks have taste buds all over the inside of their mouth and throat, not just on the tongue. Some sharks also have whiskery feeler-like tentacles called barbels that have taste buds on the ends that allow them to taste and "feel" prey.

DO SHARKS GIVE BIRTH TO LIVE YOUNG?

Lemon sharks are one of the few shark species that give birth to live young. Their litters can contain up to 17 pups. The pups develop inside their mother, and an umbilical cord brings them oxygen and nutrients.

DO SHARK MOTHERS LOOK AFTER THEIR BABIES?

Shark mothers abandon their babies, but they give them a good start in life. They have their pups in shallow, coastal waters, where they will be safe during their early years.

WHAT DOES A BABY SHARK LOOK LIKE?

Most sharks develop inside eggs inside their mother's body, not connected to her by an umbilical cord or placenta. When they are fully developed, the babies "hatch" and are born. Sometimes the newborn pups are still attached to their yolk sac, which provides them with food.

WHY IS IT BAD NEWS TO BE A SHARK TWIN?

A female tiger shark carries several babies during pregnancy but only gives birth to one. In the womb, the strongest baby eats the others until it is the only one left.

WHAT IS THE BIGGEST FISH IN THE WORLD?

The whale shark is the largest fish alive, growing to around 18m (59ft) long.

DO SHARKS CLOSE THEIR EYES WHEN THEY BITE?

Some sharks have a third eyelid that draws across the eye to protect it when the shark bites. Others simply roll their eyeballs up at the moment of biting.

DID YOU KNOW?

Some of the items found inside sharks' stomachs include a horse's head, a porcupine, parts of bicycles and cars, a sheep, a chicken coop—and even a suit of armor with the remains of a French soldier inside!

CAN SHARKS SEE IN THE DARK?

Unlike other fish, sharks can dilate (widen) their pupils to control how much light enters the eye. They can also make the most of the light in dim conditions, thanks to a mirror at the back of the eye, like cats' eyes. This gives sharks good vision in murky waters.

WHY ARE SOME SHARKS BLIND?

Most Greenland sharks are blinded by parasites called copepods that fix themselves to the sharks' eyes. However, the copepods produce light that attracts prey, so it doesn't really matter that the sharks can't see!

WHAT'S SPECIAL ABOUT A SHARK'S NOSE?

Sharks have special organs in their snouts that detect the electric fields produced by other living creatures.

DID YOU KNOW?

The washed-up, empty egg case of a dogfish, skate, or shark is called a mermaid's purse. The egg cases harden in the water and protect the growing embryo for six to 12 months. Then, the pup swims out of the case.

DO SHARKS SEE IN BLACK AND WHITE?

Not all sharks' eyes are the same, but most only see the world in monochrome (black and white).

WHAT DO SHARKS FEEL LIKE?

A shark's skin is covered in sharp, tooth-like scales called denticles, which feel like sandpaper. The denticles reduce drag. Throughout the shark's life, old denticles drop off and are replaced by new ones.

ARE MOST SHARKS DANGEROUS?

Even though there are more than 500 known species of shark in the world, only about 12 are actually dangerous to humans. Most attacks are accidents when a shark mistakes a human for another animal.

WHY DON'T SHARKS HAVE BONES?

For millions of years sharks have developed separately from bony fish. They grew skeletons made of cartilage rather than bone. Cartilage is the same material that holds our ears and noses in shape. It is lighter and more flexible than bones, giving sharks the ability to move in a quick and fluid way.

DID YOU KNOW?

While most fish use gas-filled swim bladders for buoyancy (staying afloat), a shark uses its liver for the same purpose.

HOW GOOD IS SHARK HEARING?

Sharks can pick up low-frequency sounds best and are more likely to react to irregular sounds—the sorts of sounds produced by an injured animal thrashing about. Sound is often the first thing that alerts sharks to prey.

HOW GOOD IS A SHARK'S SENSE OF SMELL?

Sharks use smell to find a mate and to navigate, but most of all to track down prey. They show interest in certain smells—such as blood—and totally ignore others.

HOW DOES A SHARK SMELL?

As a shark swims, seawater flows through its nostrils—the two flaps of skin at the end of its snout—and on to the nasal sacs behind. These sacs have sensory cells that can detect scents and send messages to the shark's brain.

ARE SHARKS REALLY SENSITIVE TO BLOOD?

They can't distinguish between as many different smells as we can, but they are very sensitive to certain smells. They can sense one drop of blood in a million drops of water, or a small amount of blood in water over 0.4km (quarter of a mile) away.

WHAT IS A LATERAL LINE?

Sharks have a line of sensory cells running along each side of their head and body. Water swishes over these lines of cells as sharks swim, sending signals to their brain about pressure changes and movement in the water.

WHAT DOES A LATERAL LINE DO?

The lateral line allows sharks to build up a clear "picture" of their surroundings—and to notice changes to the usual currents. Sharks can pick up the vibrations produced by a thrashing fish from 100m (328ft) away!

DO SHARKS HAVE A SIXTH SENSE?

Sharks have small pits, or openings, around their nose called ampullae of Lorenzini. These can sense electrical signals from about 50cm (20in) away. Moving muscles produce electricity, so this sense helps sharks target their prey even more precisely.

DID YOU KNOW?

In an effort to get them to mate, a German aquarium plays love songs to its sharks!

ARE SHARKS THE ONLY ANIMALS THAT SENSE ELECTRICAL SIGNALS?

No. Their close cousins, rays, have this ability too, and so do some other aquatic animals, including electric eels, some dolphins, and platypuses.

WHAT IS A SHARK'S TOP FIN FOR?

In scary movies, a dorsal fin poking above the surface warns us that a shark is coming. In reality, the dorsal fin acts like a stabilizer and stops the shark from rolling in the water.

WHY DOESN'T A SHARK SINK?

The flow of water over sharks' pectoral (side) and pelvic (bottom) fins produces lift—just like air flowing over a plane's wing. This stops sharks from sinking. Sharks change direction by tilting their fins.

WHICH SHARK HAS A TAIL AS LONG AS ITS BODY?

The thresher shark has a tail fin that can be 3m (10ft) long, as long as its body. The shark is thought to use its tail to whip and stun prey that it then turns upon to eat.

DID YOU KNOW?

A whale shark can filter up to 1,800 metric tons (400,000 gallons) of water an hour when feeding.

DID YOU KNOW?

Some sharks can detect the smell of fish at concentrations as low as one part in ten billion.

DO SOME SHARKS REST ON THE SEA BED?

Sharks that spend most of their time on the sea bed do not need to use their fins for bursts of speed. Nurse sharks' tails have almost no bottom lobe on their tail fins. These sharks sweep their eel-like tails to and fro as they hunt for crabs and lobsters.

HOW DO SHARKS FIND THEIR WAY?

Their electrosensory perception helps them to use the Earth's magnetism like an in-built compass.

HOW DO GREAT WHITE SHARKS HUNT?

The great white's hunting method helps it kill seals without injuring itself. First, it rises up at an angle and takes a surprise bite out of its prey. Then it circles, waiting for blood loss to weaken its victim, before moving in to enjoy its meal.

WHY DO SHARKS ATTACK SURFERS?

Tiger sharks attack divers and surfers partly because they look similar to seals from beneath—and partly because tiger sharks snap up anything and everything!

HOW LIKELY ARE YOU TO BE KILLED BY A SHARK?

There are fewer than 100 shark attacks per year and only 5 to 15 fatalities. You are 250 times more likely to be killed by lightning than by a shark.

CAN SHARKS HAVE BABIES ON THEIR OWN?

Despite not having a male partner, a hammerhead shark gave birth in a zoo in Nebraska, USA, in 2001. The female shark used a type of reproduction called parthenogenesis in order to keep the species alive when no male sharks are available.

DO SHARKS HUNT IN TEAMS?

Copper sharks and silky sharks co-operate to hunt. They work together to herd fish into a ball shape called a bait ball. Then the sharks start snapping at the closely packed fish. Gray (or grey) nurse sharks work together, too. They thrash their tails to drive fish into the shallows. The action creates underwater waves that sweep the prey toward shore. Reef sharks may follow the nurse sharks to steal a share of the trapped fish.

WHAT ARE "WOLVES OF THE SEA"?

Blue sharks are sometimes called the "wolves of the sea." They spend a lot of their time as loners, but they also form schools, or groups, when they hunt. Blue sharks eat fish, squid, and seabirds.

WHAT IS A FEEDING FRENZY?

Once a group of sharks finds lots of prey, the blood in the water and the jerky movements of the fish overexcite the sharks. They might lunge at each other as well as the prey!

WHY DO BASKING SHARKS SWIM WITH THEIR MOUTHS WIDE OPEN?

Filter feeders, such as basking sharks, swim along with their huge mouths wide open. Every so often they shut their jaws, forcing seawater through the gills. Bristles called gill rakers strain food from the water and channel it into the throat.

HOW DO MEGAMOUTHS FIND THEIR FOOD?

Megamouths are mysterious sharks that live in the deep ocean. They have glow-in-the-dark spots around their mouths that seem to lure plankton and small fish.

HOW MUCH FOOD DOES A WHALE SHARK EAT?

Whale sharks and megamouths are able to vacuum up water and food. Thanks to suction power and a gaping 1.5m- (5ft-) wide mouth, a whale shark can take in enough tiny plankton to sustain its 15-metric ton (33,070lb) bulk.

DO SHARKS MIGRATE?

Yes, some do. Female blue sharks feed and mate off the east coast of North America, then travel across the Atlantic to give birth off the coast of Africa. The round trip that they make every three years or so is 15,000km (9,321 miles).

WHY DO **TIGERS SHARKS** GO FOR DINNER IN HAWAII?

Tiger sharks travel to take advantage of gluts of easy prey. The sharks arrive in the waters around Hawaii just as the albatross chicks hatch, then they continue onward to eastern Australia in time for the turtle season.

WHAT IS THE OLDEST SHARK?

Greenland sharks, which live in icy waters near the Arctic Circle, can live for hundreds of years. One shark, identified in 2016, is almost 400 years old!

DID YOU KNOW?

In just one year, lemon sharks grow more than 24,000 new teeth. That's a full set every two weeks! Who needs to bother with brushing?

WHY DO HAMMERHEAD SHARKS LOOK SO ODD?

Hammerhead sharks have wide, hammer-shaped heads with eyes on the tips. Swinging their heads from side to side gives them brilliant all-round vision. During the day, hammerheads often rest together in large groups of up to 100.

WHAT EATS SHARKS?

Sharks are apex predators, which means that they have no natural predators of their own. However, sharks are still at risk from being eaten—by other, bigger sharks!

DO CARPET SHARKS LIVE ON FLOORS?

Some sharks have mottled markings that look like carpet patterns and help camouflage them. The tasselled wobbegong is one of the strangest carpet sharks. Its seaweed-like tentacles swish in the current, disguising the shark and attracting prey.

WHAT IS A SAW SHARK?

Saw sharks are extremely rare. They have wide, flat bodies, but their distinguishing feature is a long, narrow snout studded with pointy teeth. The sharks use this "saw" to slash at fish or to probe the seabed for shellfish.

HOW DO GREAT WHITE SHARKS CATCH THEIR PREY?

Great whites sneak up on their prey from below, swimming up very fast to snatch the unsuspecting creature in their jaws.

DO WHALE SHARKS CARRY PASSENGERS?

Whale sharks don't just feed themselves—they feed hangers-on, too. Remoras are small fish that use suckers on their heads to fix themselves to whale sharks' bellies. They eat scraps that fall from the mouths of their hosts.

WERE THERE SHARKS IN THE AGE OF THE DINOSAUR?

Yes—and long before then, too. Ancestors of the shark were swimming in the world's oceans 450 million years ago, 230 million years before the first dinosaurs appeared.

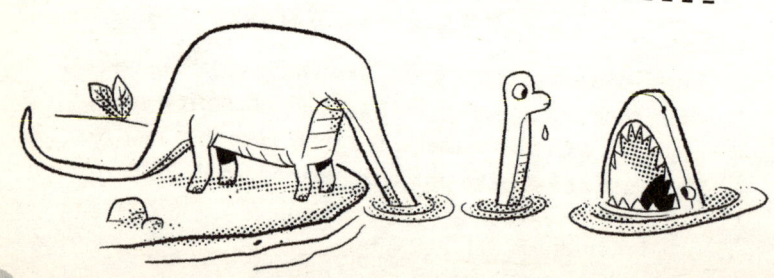

DEEPLY DIPPY

WHAT HAPPENS WHEN AN OCTOPUS LOSES AN ARM?

If an octopus loses an arm, it can grow a new one! Even after it has been cut off, an octopus arm will carry on wriggling for some time.

DID YOU KNOW?

An octopus will sometimes eat its own arms, and even its own body, if it becomes extremely stressed.

WHAT ARE LOBSTERS AFRAID OF?

Lobsters are scared of octopuses. Even the sight of one is enough to make a lobster freeze in horror.

HOW BIG IS A BABY OCTOPUS?

When a baby octopus is born, it is about the size of a flea.

DID YOU KNOW?

Some types of octopus contain a poison that instantly kills any creature that eats them.

DOES AN OCTOPUS HAVE MORE THAN ONE HEART?

Octopuses have three hearts! Two pump blood through its gills to help it breathe while the third pumps blood around the rest of its body.

CAN OCTOPUSES CHANGE SHAPE?

The mimic octopus can change its shape and shade in order to scare off predators. It has been known to make itself look like a very convincing sea snake.

DID YOU KNOW?

Octopuses have been known to remove the stinging tentacles from jellyfish and use them as weapons.

WHICH SEA CREATURE HAS THE LARGEST EYES?

The vampire squid has the largest eyes of any animal in relation to its body size. If it was the size of a human, it would have eyes the size of table tennis paddles!

WHY DID DENTISTS LIKE STINGRAYS?

Ancient Greek dentists used the venom from stingrays' spines as an anesthetic.

DID YOU KNOW?

Sharks and rays are the only animals on the planet that are immune to cancer. Scientists believe this may be something to do with their skeletons, which are made of cartilage rather than bone.

HOW DOES A STINGRAY'S STING WORK?

A special cap on the end of a stingray's tail will break off when it attacks its prey. This allows even more poison to flow into its victim's wound.

HOW BIG CAN SQUID GROW?

The largest giant squid ever caught was a whopping 13m (43ft) long and weighed almost a metric ton (2,200lb). Its body was so enormous that calamari rings (squid rings) made from it would have been the size of truck tires!

DID YOU KNOW?

Instead of black ink, some species of deep sea squid squirt a cloud of glowing luminous ink to distract predators in the dark depths of the ocean.

WHERE DO TURTLES LIVE?

Turtles live on every continent except Antarctica.

WHY DO LEATHERBACK TURTLES HAVE SPINY THROATS?

The spines keep their meals from escaping! They stop their preferred snack of jellyfish from sliding back out of their mouths.

DID YOU KNOW?

The jaws of a snapping turtle are so powerful that they can rip off a human finger.

HOW LONG CAN TURTLES DIVE FOR?

Green sea turtles can stay underwater for up to five hours. To achieve this, they slow their heart rate to help conserve oxygen, with up to nine minutes between heartbeats.

WHY SHOULD TURTLES AVOID MAN O' WAR JELLYFISH?

When a turtle eats a Portuguese man o' war jellyfish, the jellyfish releases a smell that attracts sharks. It's the jellyfish's way of getting revenge on the turtle!

DID YOU KNOW?

The pistol shrimp got its name from the loud banging noise it makes with its claws in order to surprise its prey.

IS THERE AN ANIMAL WITH JUST ONE EYE?

The only creature known to have just one eye is the copepod. It is a tiny crustacean that swims around in groups of up to one trillion members.

HOW DID THE ROBBER CRAB GET ITS NAME?

The robber crab got its nickname from its habit of stealing shiny things like pots and pans from people's houses! The crab is the largest and heaviest land-living crustacean, weighing up to 4.1kg (9lb). Only the females enter the sea to lay their eggs. If they stay too long, though, they drown!

WHERE CAN YOU FIND MONSTER CRABS?

The Barents Sea is teeming with monster Kamchatka crabs after they were introduced in the 1960s to provide a fishing source for Russian fishermen. The gigantic crustaceans can measure more than 1m (3ft) from claw to claw.

ARE PREHISTORIC CRABS STILL ALIVE TODAY?

Horseshoe crabs are "living fossils." They first appeared on Earth in the Carboniferous period, 300-355 million years ago. Little has changed about their appearance since then, as fossils from the late Jurassic era show.

WHAT IS THE LARGEST CRAB IN THE WORLD?

The largest of all crustaceans is the Japanese spider crab. Its body is about 37cm (15in) across but its legs are like stilts, spanning up to 3.81m (12.5ft).

WHAT IS THE WORLD'S HEAVIEST CRUSTACEAN?

The North Atlantic lobster grows up to 60cm (24in) long and can weigh up to 20kg (44lb), making it the heaviest crustacean that lives in the sea.

WHICH CRUSTACEAN IS THE FASTEST SWIMMER?

While lobsters can leap away from predators at great speed, the fastest-swimming crustacean is Henslow's great swimming crab. Most crabs catch prey by walking up to it but Henslow's crab swims after food at about 4.7km/h (2.9mph).

DID YOU KNOW?

When spiny lobsters migrate, as many as 60 individuals walk in single file along the sea bed. The wandering lobsters can travel 50km (30 miles) without a break.

IS THERE A CRUSTACEAN THAT EXPLODES?

The female fish louse—a tiny crustacean—can give birth to up to 100 babies, but she can't fit them inside her body! As the babies grow, she loses her internal organs to make space for them. When the babies are big enough, the mother explodes, releasing her young but, of course, the mother dies when this happens.

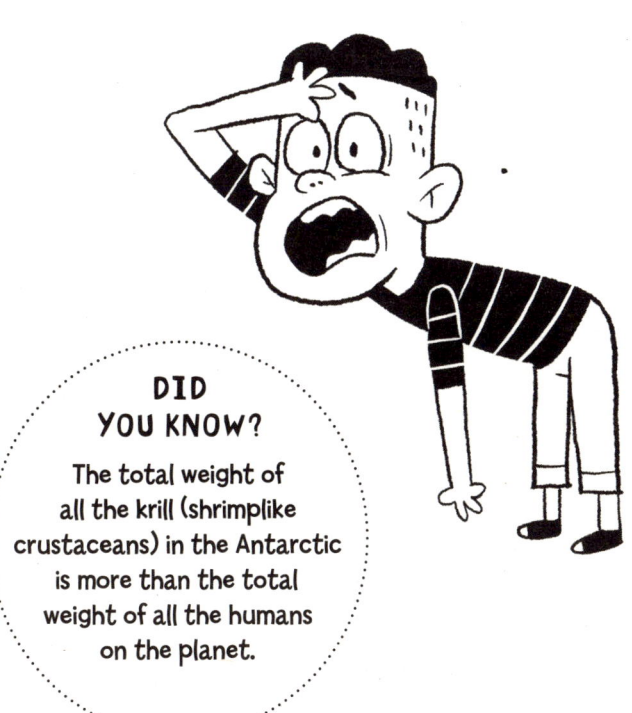

DID YOU KNOW?

The total weight of all the krill (shrimplike crustaceans) in the Antarctic is more than the total weight of all the humans on the planet.

HOW LONG CAN JELLYFISH TENTACLES GROW?

The tentacles of a lion's mane jellyfish can reach up to 36m (120ft) away from its body.

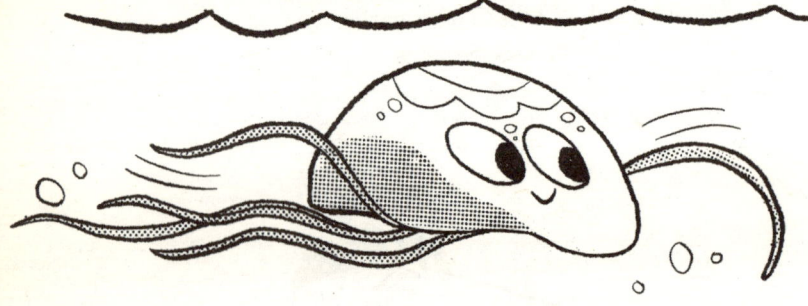

CAN JELLYFISH SWIM?

Unlike other jellyfishes, the stinging box jellyfish has many eyes, plus muscles that it uses to swim against the tide, to catch prey—and swimmers!—unaware.

HOW BIG IS THE WORLD'S BIGGEST JELLYFISH?

The largest jellyfish in the world is the Arctic lion's mane that lives in the northwest Atlantic Ocean. Its bell, or body, grows up to 2.1m (7ft) across with tentacles stretching 36.5m (120ft).

WHAT IS THE DEADLIEST JELLYFISH?

The tentacles of the deadly box jellyfish contain thousands of tiny harpoons, which inject poison into its unlucky victim. The jellyfish's body is about the size of a football, but it's the long tentacles you have to watch out for. There can be up to 60 of them, each up to 4.6m (15ft) long. These are covered with millions of venom-packed capsules. Just 3m (10ft) of tentacle wrapped around a human can deliver a fatal dose.

HOW MANY PEOPLE HAVE DIED FROM BOX JELLYFISH STINGS?

In the waters around Australia, more folks have died from box jellyfish stings than shark or crocodile attacks—about 70 people in the last century. Luckily, an antivenom was developed in 1970.

WHAT IS A JELLYFISH MADE OF?

A jellyfish is 95 percent water—the same as a cucumber! Not as nice in a salad though!

WHAT DO YOU CALL A GROUP OF JELLYFISH?

A group of jellyfish is called a "smack."

DID YOU KNOW?

If you spread them out, the tentacles of an Arctic jellyfish would stretch over 15 tennis courts.

HOW LONG IS A MORAY EEL?

The slender giant moray eel has been known to grow to nearly 4.5m (15ft) in length.

DID YOU KNOW?

The moray eel has two sets of teeth in its throat; the first set bites the eel's prey, while the second set moves up into the eel's mouth and locks on more tightly. The first set then moves to pull the prey down the eel's throat.

HOW DO YOU ESCAPE A MORAY EEL?

If you're bitten by a moray eel, the only way to get away is to kill it by cutting off its head and breaking its jaws. It won't let go while it's alive.

HOW SHOCKING IS AN ELECTRIC EEL?

Electric eels can deliver a shock of 500 volts to stun their prey into submission. The electricity supplied to your home is only 240 volts! You could power two fridges with the electricity produced by a single electric eel.

DID YOU KNOW?

The lamprey, an eel-like creature, has no jaws. To eat, it attaches its sucker mouth to another fish then literally sucks all the fluids out of it, killing the fish by sucking it dry.

CAN EELS CLIMB UP WALLS?

Glass eels are always determined to get to their destination and have been known to climb up the wet walls of dams to get around an obstacle in their way.

HOW BRAINY IS A SEA STAR?

A sea star doesn't have a brain. An extremely complex nerve system called the nerve plexus controls its arms instead.

HOW DOES A SEA STAR EAT?

A sea star can turn its stomach inside out by pushing it through its mouth.

DID YOU KNOW?

Giant sea stars are starfish that can have an arm span of more than 60cm (24in). They can be brown, green, red, or orange.

WHAT IS A MANATEE'S CLOSEST RELATIVE?

The closest living relatives to the manatee are actually elephants and hyrax.

HOW DO WALRUSES SLEEP IN THE SEA?

Walruses fill an inflatable throat pouch called a pharyngeal with air to keep them afloat while they sleep.

DID YOU KNOW?

Odobenus rosmarus, the scientific name for a walrus, is Latin for "tooth-walking sea-horse."

IS THERE A SEA UNICORN?

The long horn of the narwhal is actually an extended tooth! Its other name, "unicorn of the sea," isn't really correct, because it has no horn!

DID YOU KNOW?

The gray (or grey) seal's scientific name, Halichoerus grypus, comes from the Greek meaning "hook-nosed sea pig."

WHICH FISH IS LIKE A VACUUM CLEANER?

Some grouper fish are so huge that when they open their mouths they create a suction that pulls prey straight into their gaping maws.

WHERE IS THE WORLD'S LARGEST REEF?

The Great Barrier Reef, off the east coast of Australia, is the world's largest coral reef, home to five percent of the world's fish species. It is the biggest single structure made by animals. It was created over thousands of years by tiny animals called coral that form a rocky skeleton.

DID YOU KNOW?

When parrotfish munch on hard coral to get at tasty algae, the coral is pooped out as white sand. The fish are responsible for dumping tons of sand around reefs every year.

DOES A PARROTFISH HAVE A BEAK?

This fish has a beak like a parrot, but it can't talk! Parrotfish use their beaks to scrape algae off rocks and corals.

WHY SHOULD DIVERS WATCH WHERE THEY STEP?

Is it a piece of weed-covered rock or a fish? Stonefish are disguised to look like stones lying on the seabed. This camouflage hides them from prey and predators, such as bottom-feeding sharks and rays.

ARE STONEFISH DANGEROUS?

Stonefish have a row of needle-like spines on their back that can inject deadly venom. Stonefish venom can kill a person within two hours—unless he or she is treated in time with antivenom.

WHICH FISH WRESTLES WITH ITS MOUTH?

Jawfish have outsized jaws. They fight one another in mouth-wrestling competitions.

HOW DOES A JAWFISH LOOK AFTER ITS EGGS?

Jawfish are mouth brooders. They look after their eggs inside their mouths until they hatch.

DID YOU KNOW?

The jawfish also tunnels with its mouth. It scoops up a mouthful of sand and transports it elsewhere, gradually hollowing out a home.

WHICH FISH MAKES ITS OWN ANTIFREEZE?

The Arctic cod can survive in waters around the north pole that would otherwise turn them to ice cubes. They create an antifreeze protein in their bodies that stops ice crystals from forming in their blood so it stays liquid.

DOES A SWORDFISH SPEAR ITS PREY?

Swordfish have long, pointed bills that look like swords. While prey could get caught on its tip, the swordfish could never reach it with its jaws. It uses the "sword" to slash and injure its prey before grabbing it in its teeth.

IS THERE A DEADLY SNAIL IN THE SEA?

Yes! The cone snail, which lives in the waters of the Indo-Pacific, is a venomous gastropod that injects venom using a disposable dart. The geographer cone is the deadliest cone snail. The venom can cause nausea, dizziness, and sometimes paralysis and death!

CAN DIVERS GET TRAPPED UNDERWATER BY GIANT CLAMS?

Not really. Many adventure movies show divers getting a leg trapped in the closing shell of a giant clam but, while you could fit a leg in some huge bivalve specimens, they close their shells so slowly that most sensible divers could retract a limb before it gets stuck. Which begs the question—what were you doing sticking a leg in a giant clam?!

HOW FAST DO GIANT CLAMS GROW?

Not very fast at all. One North Atlantic deep-sea clam studied by Yale University scientists was estimated to take 100 years to grow about 8mm (0.3in)!

DID YOU KNOW?

The crevalle jack (a type of fish) is capable of producing croaking sounds by grinding its teeth together while releasing gas from its swim bladder.

DO ALL OYSTERS HIDE PEARLS?

No. True natural, round pearls are very rare, as they are created by accident. Most pearls sold in shops are grown in specialized pearl-oyster farms.

HOW BIG WAS THE BIGGEST NATURAL PEARL?

The largest pearl found in the wild was discovered in a giant clam off the coast of Palawan in the Philippines in 1934. The "Pearl of Lao Tzu" weighed 6.4kg (14lb 2oz) and measured 24.1cm (9.5 in) across. It sold at auction in 1980 for $200,000.

HOW ARE PEARLS MADE?

When a pearl oyster senses a parasite or irritant in its shell, it forms a sac around it as a defense. Minerals form around the sac to create a coating of shiny nacre, or mother-of-pearl.

ARE SPONGES ANIMAL OR PLANTS?

Sponges are animals, very primitive ones, that attach themselves to the sea floor. Sponges have many cells, but don't have any organs. They draw water into their bodies through pores and filter it for food and oxygen.

HOW ANCIENT ARE SPONGES?

Sponges were the first many-celled organisms to appear on Earth about 570 million years ago. So, quite ancient, then.

CAN SPONGES GROW FROM BROKEN PIECES OF THEIR BODY?

Yes. A sponge can regenerate from a tiny piece of itself. If you pushed a sponge through a sieve, the individual parts could float away and grow into new sponges.

CAN SEA STARS GROW NEW ARMS?

Yes. All sea stars can grow a new arm if one is lost or bitten off. Some can even grow half their body back, with the two parts regenerating into two separate sea stars!

CAN A SEA STAR GROW BACK FROM A TINY PIECE?

One amazing sea star, in the family Ophidiasteridae, can grow a new body from just a 1cm (0.38in) piece of arm. It can take a year for this to happen, though.

WHY ARE SEA STARS RUINING REEFS?

Spiny sea stars called crown-of-thorns are gobbling up coral reefs. These large, crawling creatures, up to 60cm (24in) across, can eat through half their size in coral in an evening. Large groups of them have been munching on the Great Barrier Reef and reefs in the Red Sea, Indian Ocean, and Pacific. Their spines also contain venom, so they are not easy to get rid of.

DARKEST DEPTHS

HOW MUCH DO WE KNOW ABOUT DEEP-SEA CREATURES?

More than 50 percent of all creatures brought up from the deep sea by scientists are unknown species.

WHICH FISH CAN EAT PREY BIGGER THAN ITSELF?

The deep sea gulper eel can open its mouth so wide that its jaws can bend back at a 180-degree angle. This allows it to eat fish larger than itself.

DID YOU KNOW?

If pulled out of the sea by fishermen, the quick change in water pressure makes the gases inside a Pacific grenadier fish expand. Its stomach pops out of its mouth as a result!

WHICH FISH HAS SEE-THROUGH TEETH?

The viperfish has transparent, extra-long, razor-like teeth that cannot be seen in the dark, but it has to open its jaws almost vertically to catch prey. The teeth of a viperfish are half the length of its head, so it can't close its mouth either! It has to open its jaws very wide in order to swallow.

HOW DOES A VIPERFISH CATCH ITS PREY?

The viperfish catches its prey by swimming straight toward its target and spearing it on its long teeth.

HOW DOES A VIPERFISH DEAL WITH A BIG MEAL?

The viperfish can move all of its internal organs toward its tail when it needs to make room for a large meal, with its stomach stretching to twice its normal size.

DID YOU KNOW?

Some creatures thrive in the most inhospitable places. In the darkness of the deep ocean, colonies of Pompeii worms live on boiling-hot volcanic vents, like steaming chimneys on the sea bed. Named after the site of a disastrous volcanic eruption in ancient Rome, the worms build crusty tubes to live in and poke their heads out to feed on bacteria.

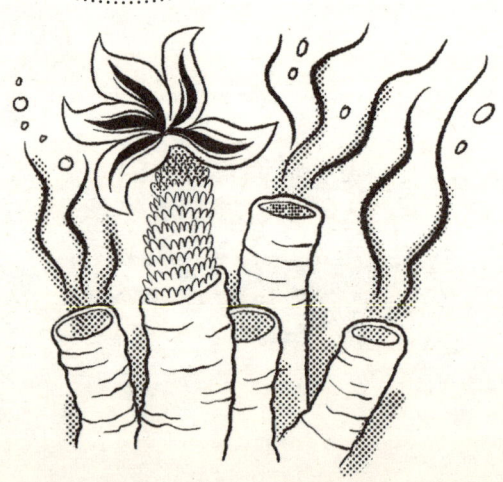

WHICH FISH CARRIES ITS OWN LAMP?

The anglerfish lives in the darkest depths of the sea and has a glowing blob, like a little lantern, dangling in front of its head! The deep-sea anglerfish's lure glows in the dark, so it can be seen through the gloom and tempt prey to come near.

HOW ATTACHED ARE MALE ANGLERFISH TO THEIR MATES?

Some male anglerfish live like parasites on the body of a much bigger female. She may carry as many as six males at a time.

WHICH IS THE GROSSEST FISH OF ALL?

Read on at your own peril—you have been warned! The slime eel, also known as the hagfish, feeds on dead and dying fish at the bottom of the sea. It has a circular mouth full of tiny, triangular teeth. After slipping through a dead creature's mouth, or eye socket, the eel eats the insides of the creature, leaving only a bag of skin and bones behind.

DID YOU KNOW?

When under attack, a hagfish produces slimy mucus, which makes the water around it turn into jelly that is impossible for predators to swim through.

CAN FISH GLOW IN THE DARK?

Some fish live so deep in the sea that sunlight can't reach them and they swim in complete darkness. Many species make their own light using a chemical reaction called bioluminescence.

WHICH FISH HAS TEETH TOO BIG FOR ITS MOUTH?

Thanks to its long, needlesharp teeth, the fangtooth is one of the fiercest-looking fish in the deepest parts of the ocean. When it shuts its mouth, the fangtooth stores its longest lower fangs in two special sockets on either side of its brain.

HOW LAZY IS A BLOBFISH?

The blobfish doesn't move much. Instead it sits and waits for its food to drift by. This 30cm (12in) fish lives in deep waters off Australia. It eats pretty much any small morsel that floats by.

CAN YOU EAT BLOBFISH?

Scientists don't know much about the blobfish—except that it's under threat. It's inedible but trawlers net it while fishing for crabs and lobsters.

DO BLOBFISH FLOAT?

The blobfish's jelly-like flesh is slightly lighter than water. This means the fish can float just above the seabed without expending any energy.

WHERE IS THE DEEPEST PART OF THE SEA?

The Mariana Trench in the western Pacific Ocean is the deepest area of the world's seas. Its maximum depth is 10.98km (6.83 miles). If you placed Mount Everest there, its peak would still be over 2km (6,561ft) below sea level.

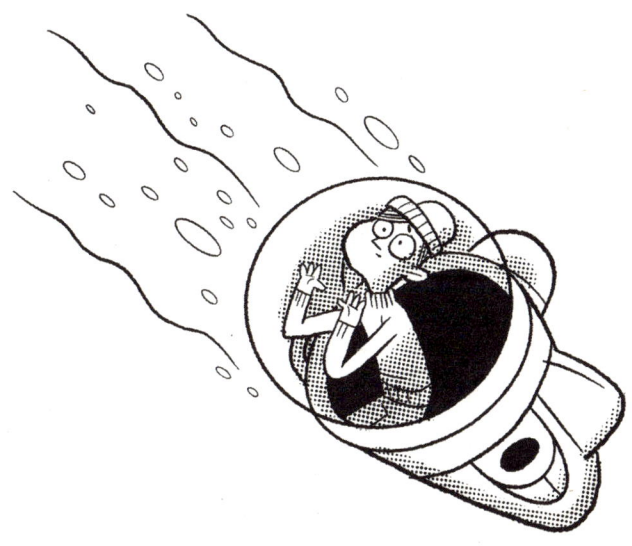

HAS ANYONE EVER BEEN THERE?

Only three people have ever dived that deep. The first dive was in the US Navy bathyscaphe Trieste in 1960, with Don Walsh and Jacques Piccard aboard. In 2012 the Canadian movie director James Cameron made the trip in the submersible Deepsea Challenger.

HOW EASY IS IT TO GET TO THE BOTTOM OF THE MARIANA TRENCH?

The pressure at such a depth is enormous, about 1,000 times the atmospheric pressure at sea level, and the temperature just above freezing. The Deepsea Challenger submersible needed steel walls 64mm (2.5in) thick to hold it together and keep the pressure constant for its pilot. The journey to the bottom of the trench took two hours and 37 minutes.

CAN ANY SEA CREATURES SURVIVE IN THE MARIANA TRENCH?

Surprisingly, yes. Divers and remotely controlled underwater vehicles have spotted snailfish near the bottom and what could have been a sea cucumber.

WHICH SEA CREATURE HAS THE BEST NIGHT VISION?

The Gigantocypris is a deep-sea crustacean with a round body made of 95 percent water. It appears more like a jellyfish than other crustaceans, such as crabs or shrimp. The Gigantocypris can see in the darkness at the bottom of the sea thanks to a pair of parabolic mirrors that reflect what little light there is back to its retinas. Despite this adaptation, the images the Gigantocypris sees are probably quite blurred.

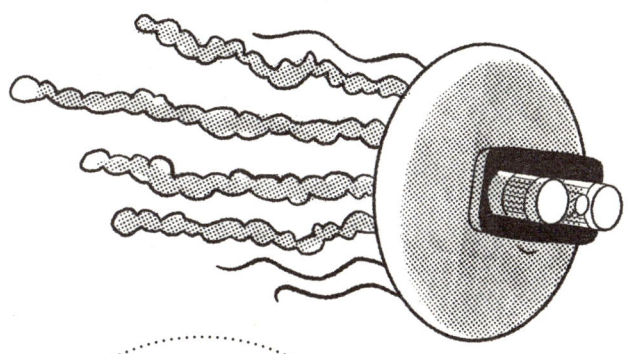

DID YOU KNOW?

The pelican eel is a deep-sea weirdo. It's named for its elastic mouth, which resembles a pelican's stretchy throat. The fish's gaping mouth is about 25cm (10in) long. The rest of its body is snakelike.

ARE THERE DRAGONS IN THE DEEPEST OCEANS?

There is a very spooky creature called the Pacific blackdragon. This 38cm (15in) predator has a snakelike body lit up by photophores on its belly. It waves a small lure from its lower jaw, and when prey comes near, it opens its mouth to reveal a ring of long, sharp fangs. The blackdragon is black on the inside too, so if it swallows luminous fish, they don't glow through its belly!

IS THERE REALLY A VAMPIRE SQUID FROM HELL?

Yes, kinda. A tiny, red creature that looks like a squid with webbing between its arms and glowing eyes has been filmed swimming in the deepest oceans. Commonly known as a vampire squid, its Latin name Vampyroteuthis infernalis does translate as "vampire squid from hell"!

SOMETHING'S FISHY

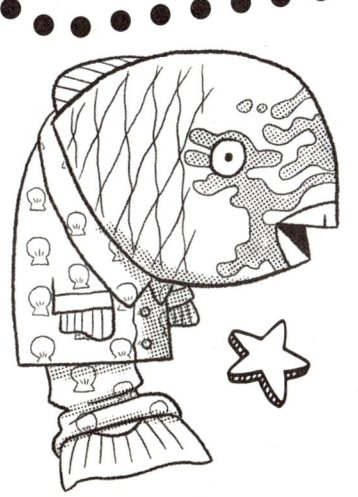

WHAT IS THE WORLD'S LARGEST BONY FISH?

The ocean sunfish is no beauty, but it is the world's heaviest bony fish. It starts life the size of a sesame seed, but eventually weighs about 1,000kg (1 ton).

HOW MANY EGGS DOES AN OCEAN SUNFISH PRODUCE?

Ocean sunfish females produce more eggs than any other vertebrate—as many as 300 million at a time! How would you like that many brothers and sisters?

WHY IS IT CALLED A SUNFISH?

The sunfish is named for its habit of "sunbathing" at the surface. It may do this to encourage seagulls to land and pick off parasites!

HOW FAST ARE SEAHORSES?

Seahorses are no good for racing, unlike horses on land. With only a small dorsal fin to flutter and push it along, it can take half an hour for a seahorse to swim the length of a human arm.

DO MALE SEAHORSES GET PREGNANT?

Yes! The babies grow for three weeks in a pouch before the male gives birth to up to 200 of them over 72 hours. The effort leaves him looking drained—unsurprisingly!

DID YOU KNOW?

Seahorses can see in two directions at once, as their eyes can move independently of each other.

CAN FISH WALK?

The rosy-lipped batfish isn't a good swimmer, but has modified fins that allow it to walk across the seabed. They make it look like it has legs! The fish has red "lipstick" that helps other rosy-lipped batfish recognize it at spawning time.

DID YOU KNOW?

Unlike other fish, a seahorse swims in an upright position. It also has no scales.

HOW DO ROSY-LIPPED BATFISH HUNT?

The batfish has a lure of frilly flesh on its forehead that tempts prey close enough to eat.

DO PARROTFISH CHANGE SEX?

Parrotfish change their patterns at different stages of their development. Most parrotfish start out female and later change into males. Imagine that!

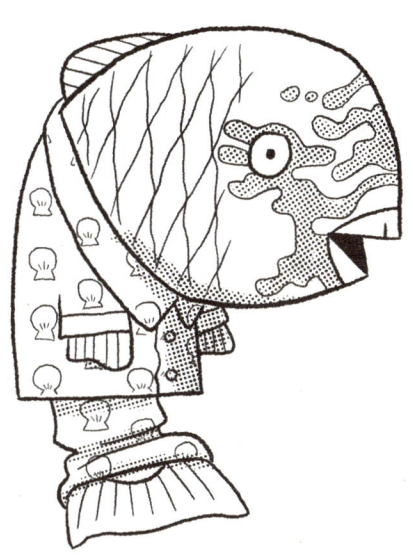

WHAT DO PARROTFISH WEAR AT NIGHT?

At night, parrotfish wrap up their body in a coating of mucus. Scientists think it makes them more difficult for eels and other hunters to sniff out and helps keep parasites away.

HOW DO FROGFISH HIDE FROM PREDATORS?

Frogfish live in warm, shallow seas. Some can change shade to match their surroundings. Some blend in with the seabed and others with their bright coral-reef surroundings.

DO FROGFISH LEAP?

No, but frogfish have leg-like pectoral fins. They use these to crawl slowly across the seabed.

WHAT ARE THE STRANGEST FROGFISH?

The hairy frogfish is a shaggy-looking beast. It feeds on flounders and other flatfish. Another, called the psychedelic frogfish, was discovered off the coast of Indonesia in 2008. Its pattern matches the stripy corals where it lives.

WHICH FISH IS THE MOST VENOMOUS?

The Indian stonefish is said to be the most venomous fish. Easy to mistake for a rock, this camouflaged creature has spines that inflict extremely painful wounds, even through a beach shoe. The effect of being injected by this fish's venom is often fatal.

ARE THERE ANY VENOMOUS SHARKS?

You would think sharks would be scary enough, with their jaws full of jagged teeth, but two species are venomous too! The spiny dogfish and Port Jackson shark are both quite small, at 1.5m (5ft), but they have venomous spines on the front of their dorsal fins.

ARE ANEMONES PLANTS OR ANIMALS?

Sea anemones are predatory animals related to corals and jellyfish. They attach themselves to a reef with a sticky foot, then filter the water with a ring of tentacles. The tentacles hide stinging cells that can paralyze small fish or crabs before they drag the food into their mouth.

WHY DO CLOWNFISH LIVE INSIDE ANEMONES?

Clownfish are immune to anemone toxin so they can use the anemone as a safe location to lay eggs. The clownfish also feed on scraps of food left by the anemone.

WHAT DO ANEMONES GAIN FROM THIS RELATIONSHIP?

Clownfish help protect the anemone from predators. Anemones can also feed on the clownfish's poop!

HOW DOES A PUFFERFISH DEFEND ITSELF?

Pufferfish can puff up like a balloon. This defense makes them too much of a mouthful for most predators—especially since many species are covered in prickles. Oh, and they're poisonous, too!

CAN YOU EAT PUFFERFISH?

In Japan, the poisonous flesh of the pufferfish—fugu—is a delicacy. Only trained chefs can prepare it.

HOW DO PUFFERFISH CATCH THEIR PREY?

Pufferfish rely on sight to find their food. They can move each eye independently.

WHAT IS THE WORLD'S LONGEST BONY FISH?

The four species of oarfish are true monsters of the deep. The giant oarfish is the world's longest bony fish. It usually grows to about 9m (30ft), but there have been reports of fish as long as 17m (55ft).

DO OARFISH COME TO THE SURFACE?

Very rarely. They don't have strong muscles and struggle to survive in choppy waters and strong currents near the surface.

WHERE CAN YOU FIND OARFISH?

Oarfish spend most of their time in deep water. They sometimes swim in an upright pose.

IS THERE A FISH THAT CAN BREATHE ON LAND AND IN WATER?

Most fish soon die if they are taken out of the water—but not the mudskipper. It can breathe on land as well as under water.

HOW DO MUDSKIPPERS BREATHE AIR?

Mudskippers take in oxygen from the air through their skin. They also save bubbles of air in their gills.

WHERE DO MUDSKIPPERS LIVE?

Mudskippers live in coastal regions. When the tide goes out, they walk or skip around the mud flats looking for food.

DO FLYING FISH ACTUALLY FLY?

Flying fish have a neat trick for escaping marine predators—they leave the water! Swimming at top speed, the fish can break the surface and glide through the air.

WHAT DO FLYING FISH USE FOR WINGS?

The fish glide on stiff, outstretched pectoral fins. Their average gliding speed is about 16km (10 miles) per hour.

HOW FAR CAN FLYING FISH GLIDE?

A flying fish can cover up to 180m (590ft) in a single glide.

ARE ANY PREHISTORIC FISH STILL ALIVE?

For a long time scientists only knew about coelacanths from fossils. They thought they had become extinct millions of years ago. But then in 1938 a live coelacanth was caught!

DID YOU KNOW?

If you kept a goldfish in a darkened room for long enough, it would eventually turn white.

HOW LONG IS A COELACANTH PREGNANCY?

Coelacanth eggs develop inside the mother's body perhaps for as long as three years. Then, the mother gives birth to five or more well-developed young.

DID YOU KNOW?

An oyster can change its sex several times during its life!

DO ANY FISH LIVE IN MUD?

A killifish embryo can survive in mud, with no water or oxygen, for more than 60 days.

COULD FISH SURVIVE IN A TANK OF HUMAN BLOOD?

Most tropical marine fish could survive in a tank filled with human blood due to the amount of oxygen it contains.

HOW MANY DIFFERENT KINDS OF FISH ARE THERE?

So far, around 32,000 species of fish have been identified, compared with only 6,400 species of mammal.

WHERE DO MOST OF THE FISH LIVE?

Less than 0.1 percent of Earth's water is fresh water, yet it is home to a whopping 40 percent of all fish species.

DID YOU KNOW?

When fully grown, the Philippine goby fish is only 0.7cm (0.3in) long. That's smaller than your little fingernail!

WHAT IS THE MOST TOXIC THING IN THE SEA?

The most toxic natural poison in the world comes from a piece of coral. The poison of the Palythoa can kill a rabbit with only a 25-nanogram injection; 4 micrograms can kill a human. Death occurs within minutes and there is no known antidote.

DID YOU KNOW?

When it has eaten as much as it can, a barracuda will herd any remaining fish that it has not eaten into shallow water. It guards them until it is ready to eat again.

IS THERE A SEE-THROUGH FISH?

A glassfish is completely transparent, so you can see all its bones and internal organs without cutting it open.

WHY ARE THERE NO YELLOWMOUTH BABY BOYS?

All yellowmouth grouper fish are born female. As they grow, they change into males, but only a small percentage ever survive long enough to make the change.

DID YOU KNOW?

Stargazer fish are like super electric eels. As well as delivering electric shocks, they also have two poisonous spines on their backs. Scary!

DO TUNA FISH EVER REST?

Tuna fish swim constantly for their entire lives. Over 15 years, a single tuna will cover a distance of around 1.6 million km (1 million miles).

WHAT DOES A BARRACUDA EAT FOR ITS LAST MEAL?

A dying barracuda fish will gorge itself on anything that will make its flesh poisonous, such as small creatures and plants. That way, anything that eats the barracuda after it dies will also be killed. Nasty!

DID YOU KNOW?

Some fish can get seasick.

HOW MANY EGGS DOES A COD LAY?
A female cod can lay up to nine million eggs in a single pregnancy.

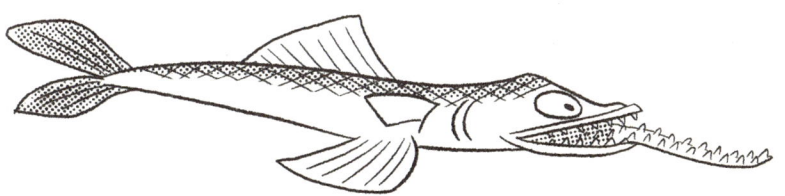

WHICH FISH HAS TEETH ON ITS TONGUE?
Lizardfish are bottom-dwelling fish with a mouth full of sharp teeth, even on their tongues!

WHY ARE CATFISH EXTRA TASTY?
A catfish has ten times as many taste buds as a human.

CAN FISH SURVIVE IN VERY SALTY WATER?

The desert pupfish, found in isolated pools in Death Valley, USA, can survive in water three times saltier than the ocean. It can also endure temperatures of more than 38°C (100°F).

WHAT'S THE OLDEST ANIMAL EVER FOUND?

A quahog clam found off the coast of Iceland in 2007 has been identified as being between 405 and 410 years old, making it the oldest animal ever discovered. It was a baby when Elizabeth I was on the throne in England (1558-1603), and was nearly 350 years old by the end of World War II!

WHICH FISH CAN GET A JOB IN A HEALTH SPA?

Some health spas use garra rufa fish to treat skin problems. People sit in shallow pools filled with the fish, then wait for their dead skin and scabs to be nibbled away!

WHY SHOULD YOU NEVER WALK A DOG NEAR A CERTAIN GERMAN LAKE?

In 2001, a giant catfish in a park lake in Germany became known as "Kuno the killer" after it jumped out and ate a Dachshund puppy—whole!

DID YOU KNOW?

The flying gurnard swims in water, walks on land, and flies through the air ... and most unbelievable of all, it's a fish!

WHY SHOULDN'T YOU EAT A BLUE TANG?

Despite its beautiful looks, the flesh of the blue tang fish is actually poisonous if eaten by humans or other fish.

HOW BIG CAN CLAMS GROW?

The tridacna clam has been known to grow up to 1.2m (4ft) long and weigh up to 227kg (500lb). Not bad for a clam!

CAN ANY FISH WALK ON DRY LAND?

The Asian climbing perch can "walk" on land in search of water when its water source dries up. It uses its fins and tail to pull itself along the ground.

HOW FAST IS A SAILFISH?

The cosmopolitan sailfish can swim faster than a cheetah can run! It can swim 109km (68 miles) per hour— that's 9km (6 miles) faster than a cheetah's top speed.

DID YOU KNOW?

The sailfish has a dorsal fin along most of its back that can be raised like a sail when it's excited.

WHICH SEA CREATURE HAS 100 EYES?

A scallop has about 100 eyes around the edge of its shell. Very handy for spotting approaching predators!

CAN ANY FISH SURVIVE FOR YEARS OUT OF WATER?

The lungfish can live out of water for as long as four years!

DID YOU KNOW?

A sea slug can eat a hydroid (an underwater stinging nettle) without being stung. The stinging chemical is absorbed into its skin and then stings anything that tries to eat the slug. Clever!

WHAT HAPPENS WHEN YOU PLAY CHESS WITH A SOLE?

If you place a sole (a type of flat fish) on a chessboard, it will take just four minutes to change its skin patterns to match the squares on the board.

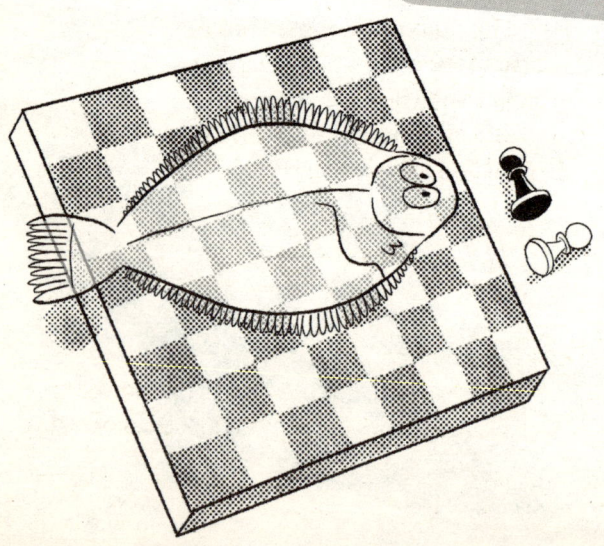

CAN FISH CHEW?

Because of the design of their jaws, fish can't actually chew—they swallow most of their food whole.

DID YOU KNOW?

In 2003, the Australian navy boarded an Indonesian ship that was drifting off the coast and found no sign of the crew or indications of an emergency. The only thing they found onboard was 3 metric tons (6,614lb) of rotting mackerel and tuna.

DO ALL FISH HAVE RED BLOOD?

Some fish in Antarctica have a natural antifreeze in their bodies which makes their blood appear white instead of red.

WHO MADE A GLOW-IN-THE-DARK GOLDFISH?

Why keep normal pet goldfish when a Taiwanese company has made a fish that glows in different shades? By injecting a protein extracted from jellyfish, the super-fish glows gold under normal light and a variety of different shades under aquarium lights.

DID YOU KNOW?

The long-nosed chimaera fish lives in the deep sea around South Africa at depths of 2,438m (8,000ft) and has a nose shaped like a fighter plane. Don't get too close, though, as a single touch from its spine is enough to kill a human.

WHY ARE HERRING LIKE SOLDIERS?

The collective name for a group of herring is an army.

WHICH FISH IS A SPITTER?

The archerfish likes to lurk near the surface of the water before spitting well-targeted jets to knock down passing flying insects and eating them. The archerfish can hit prey from a distance of 1.5m (5ft).

IS A LIONFISH DANGEROUS?

The lionfish looks beautiful, with its orange striped patterns and long fins, like feathers, sprouting all over its body, but watch out! The fins and spines on its body are for defense and are highly venomous. A sting from one of these can cause a human diver excruciating pain.

CAN ANY FISH HAVE BABIES WITHOUT PARTNERS?

Some female bony fish can produce babies without a partner. The baby is a clone of its mother.

WHICH FISH TASTES WITH TOUCH?

Catfish have tastebuds on their barbels (fleshy whiskers) which means that they can taste things by simply brushing up against them.

IS THERE A FISH THAT CROAKS?

The black drum (a type of fish found in the Gulf of Mexico) gets its name from its ability to use its large swim bladder to produce croaking or drumming sounds.

"What is it you want to talk about now, Crow?"

Eve Sophi Nebulis
Crossweil's adoptive sister. Astral mage with the strongest and greatest astral power. She heads to the Empire to fulfill her longed-for wish from a century ago.

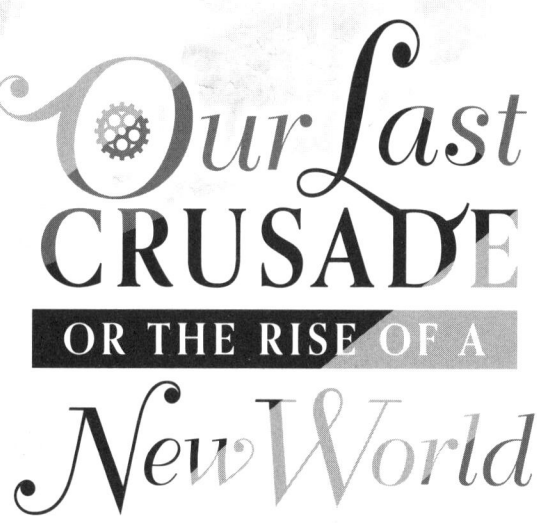

12

KEI SAZANE

Illustration by
Ao Nekonabe

NEW YORK

12 KEI SAZANE

Translation by Jan Cash
Cover art by Ao Nekonabe

This book is a work of fiction. Names, characters, places, and incidents are the product of the author's imagination or are used fictitiously. Any resemblance to actual events, locales, or persons, living or dead, is coincidental.

KIMI TO BOKU NO SAIGO NO SENJO, ARUIWA SEKAI GA HAJIMARU SEISEN Vol. 12
©Kei Sazane, Ao Nekonabe 2021
First published in Japan in 2021 by KADOKAWA CORPORATION, Tokyo.
English translation rights arranged with KADOKAWA CORPORATION, Tokyo, through TUTTLE-MORI AGENCY, INC., Tokyo.

English translation © 2023 by Yen Press, LLC

Yen Press, LLC supports the right to free expression and the value of copyright. The purpose of copyright is to encourage writers and artists to produce the creative works that enrich our culture.

The scanning, uploading, and distribution of this book without permission is a theft of the author's intellectual property. If you would like permission to use material from the book (other than for review purposes), please contact the publisher. Thank you for your support of the author's rights.

Yen On
150 West 30th Street, 19th Floor
New York, NY 10001

Visit us at yenpress.com
facebook.com/yenpress
twitter.com/yenpress
yenpress.tumblr.com
instagram.com/yenpress

First Yen On Edition: November 2023
Edited by Yen On Editorial: Shella Wu
Designed by Yen Press Design: Liz Parlett

Yen On is an imprint of Yen Press, LLC.
The Yen On name and logo are trademarks of Yen Press, LLC.

The publisher is not responsible for websites (or their content) that are not owned by the publisher.

Cataloging in Publication data is on file with the Library of Congress.

ISBNs: 978-1-9753-5026-0 (paperback)
       978-1-9753-5027-7 (ebook)

10 9 8 7 6 5 4 3 2 1

LSC-C

Printed in the United States of America

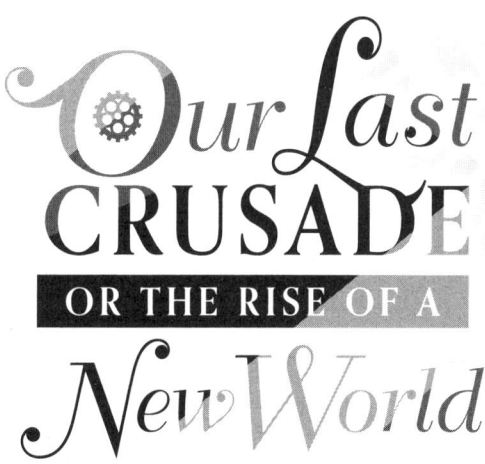

Our Last Crusade
OR THE RISE OF A
New World

So Se lu, uc song lihe thac mihas.
A love stronger than pain.

deus E gfend mihas thac elphe gfend vel hem-Ye-r-arisia Zill fears?
Do you, who fears pain more than anyone, still fear being touched and hurt?

solit kis mihas thac mihas. E yum vilis Uho.
There is something that hurts more than pain. And you will likely learn of it.

Utopia Powered by Machines
THE HEAVENLY EMPIRE

Iska
Member of Unit 907—Special Defense for Humankind, Third Division. Used to be the youngest soldier who ever reached the highest rank in the military, the Saint Disciples. Stripped of his title for helping a witch break out of prison. Wields a black astral sword to intercept astral power and its white counterpart to reproduce the last attack obstructed by its pair. An honest swordsman fighting for peace.

Mismis Klass
The commander of Unit 907. Baby-faced and often mistaken for a child, but actually a legal adult. Klutzy but responsible. Trusts her subordinates. Became a witch after plunging into a vortex.

Jhin Syulargun
The sniper of Unit 907. Prides himself on his deadly aim. Can't seem to shake off Iska, since they trained under the same mentor. Cool and sarcastic, though he has a soft spot for his buddies.

Nene Alkastone
Chief mechanic of Unit 907. Weapon-making genius. Mastered operation of a satellite that releases armor-piercing shots from a high altitude. Thinks of Iska as her older brother. Wide-eyed and loveable.

Risya In Empire
Saint Disciple of the fifth seat. Genius-of-all-trades. A beautiful woman often seen in a suit and glasses with dark green frames. Likes Mismis, her former classmate.

Paradise of Witches

THE NEBULIS SOVEREIGNTY

Aliceliese Lou Nebulis IX

Second-born princess of Nebulis. Leading candidate for the next queen. Strongest astral mage, who attacks with ice. Feared by the Empire as the Ice Calamity Witch. Hates all the backstabbing happening in the Sovereignty. Enraptured by fair fights against Iska, an enemy swordsman she met on the battlefield.

Rin Vispose

Alice's attendant. An astral mage controlling earth. Maid uniform conceals weapons for assassination. Skilled at deadly espionage. Hard to read her expressions, but has an inferiority complex about her chest.

Sisbell Lou Nebulis IX

Youngest princess of Nebulis. Aliceliese's little sister. Possesses Illumination, which reproduces footage of past events. Saved by Iska when she was captured in the Empire.

Lord Mask On

A member of the House of Zoa, which directly competes with the princesses for the throne. A conspirator whose true motives are unclear.

Kissing Zoa Nebulis

A powerful astral mage. Called the favorite child of the Zoa. Possesses astral power of thorns.

Salinger

Strongest sorcerer. Imprisoned for attempting to assassinate the queen. Currently at large.

Elletear Lou Nebulis IX

Eldest princess of Nebulis. Focused on traveling abroad. Often absent from the palace.

Our Last CRUSADE OR THE RISE OF A New World

CONTENTS

Prologue 1	1	A Sky of Shrouded Stars
Prologue 2	5	A Moonless Night
Chapter 1	11	The Day the Phantoms Disappeared
Chapter 2	27	The Song Played by the Witch on the World's Final Day: "Sorry I'm So Powerful"
Chapter 3	51	Archenemy
Intermission	117	The Covered Moon and Clouded Sun
Chapter 4	125	More Than a Prisoner, Less Than a Guest
Intermission	135	The Bent and Abandoned Thorn
Chapter 5	147	The Relationship Alice Knew Not Of
Chapter 6	169	Even if the Moon Were to Crumble
Epilogue	175	The Dream That You, the Lord, Saw
Afterword	181	

PROLOGUE 1

A Sky of Shrouded Stars

The continental railroad cut across the land. As the express train raced toward the Empire, the largest territory in the world, a girl with fair blond hair pressed her hand against the window while watching the scenery pass by.

"____"

Her sweet, serene face appeared dignified when viewed from the side. Her hair fluttered in the evening winds coming in through the slightly ajar window.

It was a picturesque scene.

If an artist happened to pass by, without a doubt, they would have made a gallant display of producing a canvas to sketch the girl.

However...

It wasn't as though a painter would happen upon her during a trip like this. Instead, an entirely different person appeared before her...

"Lady Alice, I have a report for you." An elderly servant by the name of Shuvalts had walked to her from the next train car over. The man dressed in a suit whispered so only she could hear. "The Founder has appeared in the Empire."

"…Just as we thought."

"It seems likely the Empire's seventh checkpoint was destroyed and that her battle against the Imperial forces has begun. The entire area is presently on high alert."

"…Yes, of course they would be."

She hadn't made it in time.

Aliceliese Lou Nebulis IX gritted her back teeth, frustrated by the whole situation.

……*This is like the dictionary definition of* worst-case scenario.

……*The Founder is wasting no time in burning down the Empire.*

The Empire was supposed to be her enemy. In fact, as a princess of the Nebulis Sovereignty, Alice's greatest wish was to overthrow the Empire. However, the Founder was taking it too far.

The Founder—a witch of antiquated beliefs—was likely to raze anything or anyone who got in her way along with the Empire, whether they were an Imperial or not. That would mean neutral cities in the vicinity would become casualties of her destruction as well. Untold harm would befall bystanders, which would never lead to the peace Alice wished for.

……*And Rin and Sisbell are both in the Imperial capital right now.*

……*If the Founder lays siege to the capital, they will end up victims as well. This is no joking matter!*

There was another person there as well—the swordsman Alice considered her rival was also in the capital.

"…If she touches a hair on Iska's head, I won't forgive her—even if she's the Founder."

"Excuse me?"

"Oh, it's nothing," she responded to the elderly servant and coughed to clear her throat. In any case, the Founder's attack on the capital would pose enormous problems.

PROLOGUE 1

"Shuvalts."

"Yes, Your Highness?"

"I know I've said this time and time again, but this will be the last: I will stop the Founder."

"And the Zoa as well—I know."

"Yes. I will command them in Her Majesty's place. And if they do not listen, I shall bring them back by force—even if I must tie them up with a rope and drag them back to the Sovereignty."

At that very moment, Alice was serving as the queen's proxy. Second in command only to the queen, she had the right to issue orders, and it was within her jurisdiction to give compulsory orders even to the royal family.

...... *Though the Zoa surely will not comply.*

...... *I am facing Lord Mask, after all.*

The Zoa family had all but declared they would annihilate the Empire. Unlike Alice, who wished for the mere disposal of the Imperial regime, the Zoas sought to wipe the Empire from existence. They wished for a full-scale war that would annihilate the nation.

The Zoas, who had waited all this time for the Founder's awakening, would never allow this opportunity to escape them. Even if Alice attempted to stop them, they would likely resort to any means to fulfill their plans.

"The situation seems like it will pose some difficulty..."

She released a soft sigh and raised her face to look out the window once more.

"＿＿"

"Lady Alice, you were looking outside earlier as well. Is something the matter?"

"It's just the sky."

To be more accurate, she was gazing at the blanket of clouds obscuring the night sky.

* * *

The disquieting sight of the black clouds...

The twinkling stars were obscured, which gave her a sense of foreboding. A sky of shrouded stars simply put her on edge. On this night, Alice's heart pounded especially quickly.

......*Is it from nerves?*
......*Because I need to fight against the Founder?*
She didn't know.
All she knew was that as she approached the Empire, her unease grew.

But what was it?
What was this anxiety?

PROLOGUE 2

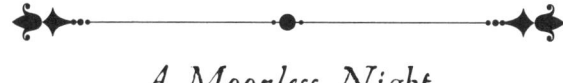

A Moonless Night

She was left with a sense of foreboding. Moonless nights were sure to bring ill tidings.

"...As if. How long am I gonna let a superstition like that affect me?"

The continental railroad cut across the land, and a gigantic wagon-like vehicle was racing down the highway that stretched alongside it. She was heading to the Imperial checkpoint.

With this Imperial vehicle and her counterfeit identification papers from her days in the Imperial forces, she would easily be able to pass through the border. She shouldn't have needed to feel anxious about anything at all, yet...

"...Something feels off."

She looked up at the night sky visible from the window. The full moon was covered by a dark, thin layer of clouds. This was the seed from which her unease sprouted. She felt apprehensive.

"**Good evening, Shanorotte,**" a man said from the communications device at the driver's seat. It was someone from the Zoa, one of the Nebulis Sovereignty's three royal families. He was Lord Mask, the current representative for the head of the household.

"**I take it your evening drive is going well?**"

"Good evening, Lord Mask. Yes, it's been very pleasant. It's so refreshing feeling the night breeze as I drive toward the horizon."

When she heard her leader's voice, the blond spy's eyes quickly softened.

Shanorotte Gregory.

Though her tone seemed easygoing, she was taller than the average adult man and had a muscular build from training. She'd used these physical traits she'd been blessed with to infiltrate the Imperial forces. The operative had risen in rank and become a commanding officer, and she had fed stolen intelligence to the Zoa family all the while.

However, her identity had been exposed during the clash to secure a vortex, and she had been on her way back to the Sovereignty. Now she was here.

"**I know it was a sudden request, but you have helped greatly by readily agreeing to the mission.**"

Lord Mask's voice was being carried by the evening wind coming in from the window. He sounded excited. She could almost imagine his pleased expression through the comm.

"**Here is the latest report: Our Revered Founder has attacked the seventh border checkpoint. Things are progressing as planned… In fact, they are going much better than anticipated.**"

"They sure are. This is the perfect opportunity to take advantage of that."

A century ago, the ancient Grand Witch had reduced the Imperial capital to a sea of flames. Her resurrection meant the entire Empire would likely be sent into a state of alarm, which was the perfect opportunity for the Zoa family.

"**Kissing and I are following after her. We are nearing the Imperial border.**"

"I'm familiar with the rendezvous point—very familiar, in fact."

"**That's right. This is your time to shine, my dear Shanorotte. I'd like you to guide us.**"

Shanorotte knew the Empire better than anyone. In fact, she was confident she knew more about the defense systems used at the border and within the cities than any Imperial, and that was all thanks to her time as an Imperial captain.

"The Zoa family will invade the capital as our Revered Founder attacks. And we will release the head of house as well as the rest of our kindred…correct?"

"**Yes, we shall. Shanorotte, where do you believe our kindred are being held?**"

"At a prison called the Divine Gallows."

It was an underground prison that detained only witches. The iron prison did not allow a single ray of light to enter, where hundreds of witches—prisoners of war—were held from the many battles fought against the Imperial forces.

"Lady Kissing's abilities should allow us to easily infiltrate the prison. Then we'll be able to quickly release our imprisoned kindred to form a powerful team of reinforcements."

"**And you believe we will be able to raze the capital to the ground then?**"

"Of course. I know the location of the prison, so simply leave the directions to me."

"**Magnificent.**"

She heard applause.

"How wonderfully reassuring, Shanorotte. Then I shall look forward to our union."

"But I must apologize, Lord Mask. I'm afraid I won't reach the border until tomorrow afternoon at the rate I'm going…"

"We shall clear the path of errant Imperial forces as we wait."

"Yes, sir."

The comm was cut off. Only the rhythmic sound of the running engine and the gathering wind remained.

"I'm glad to know Lord Mask is in a good mood for once."

She recalled the conversation. Though Lord Mask seemed to always wear a placid smile, it was simply strategic. The smile was never real.

But Shanorotte was sure his smile today had been genuine.

His long-awaited wish was about to come true. He was attempting to fulfill the Zoa family's great desire to burn the Empire to the ground, and his unrestrainable joy had been clear in his voice even through the comm.

His wish would come true soon.

Once the Founder attacked the Empire, they would take advantage of the chaos and enter the capital.

……*Yes.*

……*It really should be close at hand, yet…*

Why did she feel so uneasy?

"Hmm… I guess it's 'cause of the moon."

On the horizon ahead, the full moon had disappeared behind the dark clouds.

She didn't like this.

The moon was disappearing—and the greatest time to be a Zoa, the household of the moon, was overshadowed by the threatening clouds in the sky, by the clouds that seemed to foreshadow something.

PROLOGUE 2

"Haah... Guess what everyone says is true. I may have a large build, but my heart's small. I can't handle anxiety. I know, I know. I'm a little self-aware, at least."

The highway stretched into the horizon. Shanorotte surveyed the road leading to the Empire and exhaled.

"It should be fine. Lord Mask and Lady Kissing are here, and the Revered Founder, too. No way the moon will disappear."

CHAPTER 1

The Day the Phantoms Disappeared

1

It burst forth from deep underground in the capital.

The event was accompanied by an intense earthquake from a depth of more than two thousand meters below the surface in a hole at the Lord's office. A rumble sounded, as if the whole crust of the planet was splitting apart, and a tremor that could flip the terrain upside down surged from below.

"Again?!"

"Wh-what is this?! Why is it not stopping?!"

Their sniper, Jhin, stared at the ground as Sisbell behind him leaned against the wall. She struggled to stay standing. Even Nene and Commander Mismis, who were both trained Imperial soldiers, couldn't remain upright and narrowly managed to avoid falling over.

"Your Excellency?"

"____"

As Risya pushed up the bridge of her glasses, the silvery beastperson in front of her only looked silently at the ground. Two protruding ears stood atop the beastperson's head with a tail jutting out from their rump—this was Lord Yunmelngen.

The Lord, who was both the supreme authority of the Empire and had been the first human to make contact with astral energy a century ago, stared at the floor with wide, feline-like eyes.

"The epicenter is likely the Imperial assembly. The Eight Great Apostles must be in a hurry... I was wondering what they'd been scheming." Lord Yunmelngen's eyes narrowed. Canines flashed from the Lord's mouth as the beastperson grimaced. "I smell something very unpleasant. It's the same as the one from a century ago. I sense the dangerous power that ruined everything wafting toward us now."

The Lord continued, "So the dirty princess really did accept the calamitous power. Come with me, Black Steel's Successor."

"Uh." Iska had no idea what to say when he was abruptly called over.

The Black Steel's Successor...

He knew that a certain few within the Imperial forces called him by that name. He'd thought the nickname had originated simply from his apprenticeship under Crossweil, the Black Steel Gladiator, but his master hadn't explained the reason for the name, either.

But now he knew better.

After seeing the events of a century ago through Sisbell's Illumination power, he now learned the true reason for the name.

"Crow, what is that?"

"It's hope. We might be able to defeat the calamity at the planet's core with this."

* * *

He was the successor because the astral swords had been handed down to him.

......*But I have no idea what this calamity even is.*

......*Is it some sort of supernatural phenomenon? Or...?*

"You should see it for yourself."

The beastperson glanced at Iska as though they could see right through him.

"I will show you the enemy you'll need to face. Though the real thing isn't down there. What you'll find is simply a witch drowning in their power."

2

The Imperial assembly.

Also known as the Unseen Intent—its name originated from the diet building never being noted on any map. The space five thousand meters underground, lying in the deepest part of the Empire, once had another name.

"The Planet's Navel. That was what this excavation point was once called."

The witch's charming voice echoed all around. Her words flowed like a minstrel reciting from memory.

"Once you confirmed the existence of astral power through the old records left by the Astrals, you began your excavation five thousand meters below the surface, claiming it was a new form of energy... Well, I suppose you were right. You all are indeed wise. Until that point, you'd done the right thing."

Elletear Lou Nebulis.

The witch was no longer wearing the garments of the Lou family's first princess. Instead, she donned a jet-black wedding dress. It looked as though a cloud of dark mist had been gathered around her. Though most of her skin was left alluringly exposed by the garment, the sight of the dress still evoked a chill down one's spine.

"But what a shame. It seems you never learned from your past mistakes. You failed to contain the astral powers a century ago and caused yourselves trouble when that created the astral mages. And now, in order to acquire an even greater power, you attempted to obtain *it* as well."

"_____"

"A substance much like astral power, and also not, that the Astrals fearfully referred to as the Great Planetary Calamity. I'm sure you deeply desired it. After being reduced to nothing but mere cyberbrains, you thought that if only you had that power, you could give yourselves new forms. But look at you poor things now." She paused. Then she placed a hand on her full bosom that could even strike jealousy in the goddess of beauty herself before she continued on. "*I* was chosen by it. Not you, but me."

It was a chilling sight—her wavy emerald hair fluttered, yet there was no wind blowing. It was not because of any external force, but because of the enormous amount of power flooding out from within her.

A jet of inky blackness that obstructed all light surged from Elletear's feet.

"**Beautiful.**"

The monitors lining the wall began to speak.

"**It seems seeking the power has corrupted you. Had this been an epic poem, you would be the monster the hero would**

CHAPTER 1

slay. However, there is one thing that separates you from becoming that monster—a dream."

"A dream to create a paradise for all astral mages."

"You do not seek happiness for yourself."

"In fact, you are prepared for others to fear you, for others to believe you are a horrific witch."

"And imagine the resolve it took to abandon your godlike looks. You were willing to go to such lengths to save the weak."

"What beautiful conviction. What beautiful and lofty principles."

Applause rang out through the space. Without Luclezeus, there were only seven venerable sages, and each began to offer their opinion.

"My, how generous of you to praise me," Elletear said, shrouded in mist.

The corners of her mouth turned up. Her cold smile showed no warmth—only contempt.

"In order to show my gratitude, shall I erase you from existence *without* tormenting you, then?"

The witch had declared war.

And the Eight Great Apostles responded:

"Do you think the caged bird is happy in its confinement?"

"What did you say…?"

"We hope you enjoy your eternal stay behind bars."

The floor split.

Elletear was standing in the middle of the hall when the four corners of the assembly hall cracked apart. Warped blackish-brown towers appeared from each corner, sprouting up like plants from the ground.

"…What in the world is this?!"

Elletear's eyes widened as she looked at the four towers.

*　*　*

False Barrier—Planet's Nucleus.

Electricity discharged from the tips of the towers, enclosing the assembly floor to create an area that sealed away astral power. Simply put, it was a cage for astral power.

"We will return your words to you, Elletear."

"Perhaps it is *you* who has succumbed to your own power, *you* who has lost your original shrewdness?"

Sizzle…

As Elletear attempted to touch the barrier, sparks flew from her fingertips.

"Just as you said, you haven't eaten in more than a month, taken a sip of water in a week, and lately you haven't even needed to breathe."

"*It* has taken over your body, meaning you are no longer human, but astral power."

"Which is most favorable for us."

They could capture her. Elletear had become a mass of sinister astral power. No matter how vicious her power was, she couldn't use it in the insulated area where it had been nullified.

"We thought this might happen."

The light in the seven monitors grew stronger.

"You, an experimental subject, escaped from the scientist's compound. So we began to make preparations for the worst-case scenario."

"We anticipated you would turn on us should you successfully assimilate with it."

"And so we prepared this countermeasure."

"You flew straight into your cage, little bird."

"____"

CHAPTER 1

The barrier was like a black curtain. The beautiful woman with emerald locks who stood within it stared up at the monitors.

"Ah-ha! Ha-ha! Ah-ha-ha-ha-ha-ha!"

Suddenly, she began to laugh. The alluring giggle that passed through her bewitching lips would have struck a chill in all those who heard it.

"You think I am astral power? No, I am a witch."

Shwoo…

In that moment, smoke rose from the floor. The black current surrounded Elletear, forming something resembling a cocoon or a chrysalis.

"**What?!**"

She began to change—to evolve. The power the Eight Great Apostles had so desired that now dwelled in the princess's body was transforming her very form. She was turning from an astral mage into a monster.

"Oh, you fools."

Crick…crack…

They heard the unpleasant sound of something breaking into pieces—in fact, the piercing sound was coming from the very four towers that held her captive. Cracks had formed in the black stones, and the Eight Great Apostles could only watch as they grew bigger.

Then the towers began to break.

"**Impossible…!**"

"**We can't contain her even with this barrier?!**"

The towers collapsed. The sound of glass shattering rang as the astral-power barrier was blown to smithereens, and at its center…

A jet-black monster in human form.

* * *

A true witch.

She had turned into black particles suspended in the air, as though the night sky had condensed itself and taken on human form. She had no eyes, mouth, or nose. Hundreds of beads of light seemed to be suspended within the monster's semitransparent black body.

"I am a wicked, wicked witch, after all."

And she did not mean the type that was an astral mage. She had turned into the symbol of malice—an evil that would bring calamity to the world. Even the Eight Great Apostles, who had once witnessed the Lord's transformed and grotesque form, held their breaths as they looked upon this monster beyond all human reason. They stared at the witch, who had obtained the vilest power on the planet for herself.

"What a repulsive form…!"

"Ah-ha-ha!"

The witch spread her arms. Elletear, who had abandoned her humanity entirely, seemed in strangely high spirits as she spoke in a bewitching tone.

"Lovely. How wonderful it is to see the Eight Great Apostles so flustered when they cared not about the fear, turmoil, remorse, agony, or other pain caused while treading upon others. In fact, I'd like to broadcast this to the world… Oh my, but if I did that, I'd be exposed to the world as well. Do you think I would make children cry?"

Fwoosh!

Without warning, the monitors housing the Eight Great Apostles broke open.

The power cables connected to each of the monitors—save for the eighth one that had been Luclezeus's—fell away, and even the

CHAPTER 1

screws holding the electronics up flew off and fell to the ground. The letters *V, E, A, P, N, O,* and *W*...Vittgenshla, Etienne, Alleten, Promestius, Novalashlan, Ovan, and Wizeman—the leaders of the Empire—disappeared from the monitors.

"**Oh? Oh my, ha-ha.**" The true witch's voice rose jubilantly.

The assembly hall's wall split in half, and steam began to issue from the crack. Beyond the vapors, which were filled with the divine glitter of astral power, a silver Object rose, tearing through the wall.

"**An astralnomical soldier. Why, isn't that one of Kelvina's failed experiments? A most hideous vessel for your cyberbrains to possess.**"

The giant was half astral power and half machine. It was a pseudo-living robot that walked on two legs. Its whole form lifted and lowered as it took breaths like a real animal, and the way it bellowed out astral-energy steam was exactly like that of a living thing.

It ran on astral power.

"**We are well aware, Elletear.**"

"**The calamity in you resembles astral power, but they are actually polar opposites, like fire and water. In other words, astral energy is like poison to you right now.**"

Indeed.

In fact, Kelvina, who had become a "malevolent angel" through the calamity's power, had been eliminated in exactly that way. Iska and Rin had thrown her into an astral-power furnace.

"That element within malevolent angels and witches cannot coexist with this planet's astral power.

"So when it is exposed to a large amount of astral energy...this is the result. Astral energy doesn't have adverse effects on humans, but it's like poison to me."

* * *

Elletear was the final form of a true witch. She had turned into a being who loathed astral energy more than anything in the world.

"You, the official princess of the astral mages, will be purified by the astral energy and disappear. What a beautiful end."

"You may return to the planet from whence you came."

The giant thrust out a hand. From a cross-shaped fissure on its palm, a geyser of steam erupted, along with what seemed to be overflowing astral light. The light condensed, and before one knew it, a blinding light shot out at a speed too quick to react to.

"Nightgaze."

As the band of light flashed, it was accompanied by a high-pitched tone. The gigantic stream of light wasn't so much a beam as a pillar of pure astral energy that burned through the shadowy witch and the air itself.

Not a trace of her was left.

Nightgaze, a highly pure form of astral energy, was nearly on the scale of a midsize vortex. The light blasted everything away and left only a gigantic hole in the wall.

The assembly hall went quiet.

The wall crumbled, and the wreckage fell to the floor.

"Oh, what fun."

A beguiling laugh rang out through the space.

"Why, it was so fun that I was almost afraid. I truly despise the strong bullying the weak, but oh, I think I could get used to something as thrilling as this."

Darkness gathered in the emptiness. The witch, who had been obliterated by the beam of light, converged within a whirlwind of mist and once again formed into a humanoid shape.

"Ugh?!"

"She evaded the light?!"

CHAPTER 1

There was a murmur. Their agitation could be sensed through the gigantic soldier.

"Evade it? Of course I did no such thing. In fact, it was very painful, though I have little sense of pain now. I suppose it was similar to being doused from above with boiling water."

The witch wrapped her arms around her body.

"...So? Is that all?" She sounded indifferent.

Her declaration evoked a feeling the Eight Great Apostles hadn't experienced in a century—a chill.

"That wasn't enough. Not nearly enough. Did you truly believe such paltry astral energy could do anything to me, considering my high compatibility with this planet's calamity?"

"Impossible!"

"That was enough astral energy equivalent to that of a vortex…!"

If normal astral powers were like a rubber bullet, Nightgaze was the equivalent of a gigantic missile. And the fact that the Eight Great Apostles' beloved astralnomical soldier was unable to defeat her despite its supreme weaponry had brought the Empire's rulers fully into the realm of despair.

This meant neither the Empire nor the Sovereignty had any means of defeating Elletear.

Bullets and artillery simply wouldn't work on her. Even her singular weakness—astral energy—had no effect. She'd mocked Nightgaze for its inefficacy.

The same held true for the Sovereignty. Even if all the astral mages in the entire Nebulis Sovereignty unleashed their powers on her at once, Elletear would likely take everything directly without issue.

"You're gonna need more than that if you want to harm me at all, that is."

"Hunh?!"

"Impossible... You've already evolved this far..."

"Look, just like this."

Black lightning—that was all it could be described as—flashed as a wave of light burst forth from Elletear that easily overtook the illuminance of the Nightgaze. It hit the astralnomical soldier, and the entire contraption was blown away. Pierced by the surge of light, it broke into dozens, then hundreds of individual parts that flew through the air.

Then all those parts came falling like rain.

What was left of the soldier fell to the floor of the assembly hall in piles of debris.

"Oh, what a disappointing way to end things. I heard its armor was as strong as the planet's crust. I wonder if the royal palace's walls are this weak, too?"

She crossed her arms.

The soldier that had been looking down upon her until then was now nothing more than scraps scattered across the ground. The Eight Great Apostles within likely had been eradicated in the process as well.

"How disappointing. My dear pitiable sages, how I wish I could see you panic for longer."

She turned her back to it. She had no interest in the pile of junk strewn across the floor. The leaders who had ruled over the Empire in secret for more than a century had met an abrupt end.

"Or so it seems."

* * *

CHAPTER 1

Clatter...

Something stepped on the debris in the assembly hall. Elletear turned around and found a man standing there, holding a thin sword. The red-haired Imperial soldier wore a battle uniform that seemed to be a cross between a coat and armor.

"Oh, Joheim." The monster in human form—Elletear—let her voice ring as she addressed him. She seemed happy, delighted even. Though an Imperial soldier would have normally been an enemy, when she spoke to him, she sounded as though she was a maiden excited to see her beloved.

"**I thought you were keeping watch on the surface? Or did you come here because you were worried about me? Did you think I would lose to the Eight Great Apostles?**"

"Partially."

"?"

"Elletear, I don't know anyone smarter than you. I don't plan to play games pretending to worry about you."

The red-haired soldier walked toward her—the Saint Disciple of the first seat, the "Flash" Knight Joheim. The knight, who was part of the Imperial forces' key members and yet had sworn loyalty to Elletear in secret, stared straight ahead—looking at the astralnomical soldier's remains.

"Don't underestimate the Eight Great Apostles."

Rubble and machine parts were piled high in front of him.

He looked down upon it all.

"They survived more than a century simply to hold power over this planet. Their ambition and persistence run deep. They'd do anything to guarantee their survival. They have no such thing as dignity. Even if it means…"

Creak.

He had kicked some rubble in front of his shoe.

Underneath were fragments from the seven monitors. They were still glowing faintly even now.

"For example, they might pretend they're dead under all this rubble."

"—?!"

The monitor fragments flickered precipitously. It was clear they were still there. Their discomposure at what Joheim had said had manifested as the flickering.

"Look. Even when they've been broken to pieces like this and can't talk or project their forms, they still try to lurk. They likely planned on linking to another machine to restore themselves as soon as we left."

The Eight Great Apostles were cyberbrains, meaning they had no organic bodies.

Even without an astralnomical soldier, if they had a machine to connect to, they would be able to resuscitate themselves.

"**I'm much obliged...**" She sighed with both admiration and exasperation. "**Really now... How far will they fall? Their bodies have already come apart, yet they cling to this world as only fleeting thoughts.**"

The seven monitors flickered incessantly. It seemed as though they were begging Elletear as she looked down upon them.

"I am an evil witch. Though I have no attachment to the Sovereignty anymore...there was something I still wished to do as an astral mage. I'm sure you must know what that is, as a century ago, you were the ones who shed the blood of so many mages and caused them so much strife," said the princess of the astral mages as she peered down at the Eight Great Apostles, the seven glowing and broken monitors. "**So I will trample you to pieces in honor of the anger of all astral mages everywhere.**"

CHAPTER 1

"_____!"

"...Is what I would like to say, but it seems that won't be necessary."

She turned around instead. She beckoned for Joheim with her hand and turned her back to the remains of the astralnomical soldier. The monster in the shape of a human simply walked right out of the hall.

She left the seven splintered monitors behind.

Was she turning a blind eye to them? Were they spared?

After Elletear and Joheim had left, the hall was filled with nothing but silence.

Clatter...

A small piece of debris fell from the cracked concrete ceiling overhead.

"Ugh?!"

Yes.

From the Nightgaze that the Eight Great Apostles had discharged and Elletear's burst of astral energy, the hall was at its limit.

And it began to collapse.

It started with small fragments, building momentum until the debris grew more and more massive. Right at that moment...from out of nowhere, they heard the witch's voice.

"Good-bye, criminals of the past.

"Both the Planet's Navel and the Imperial assembly, the very symbol of authority—you've always wanted to go down together, haven't you?"

Finally, the whole thing collapsed.

* * *

Hundreds of pounds, then several tons of rubble. The ceiling crumbled, and the gray rain of pebbles crushed the seven broken monitors, leaving not a trace.

The Imperial assembly and all Eight Great Apostles disappeared from the planet.

CHAPTER 2

The Song Played by the Witch on the World's Final Day: "Sorry I'm So Powerful"

1

Once, there were siblings who went by the name of Nebulis.

The three traveled to the largest nation in the world, the Empire, to make their fortune, but they were showered in astral energy in the Planet's Navel, the deepest mining site in the world. Two of them became witches, and the third, a sorcerer.

The older twin, Eve, later became known as the Founder. The younger twin, Alicerose, as Nebulis I. And their younger brother, Crossweil, stayed in the Empire to serve the Lord as the Black Steel Gladiator.

And two of them had reunited for the first time in a century.

Imperial territory, seventh checkpoint.
The checkpoint at the nation's border was presently engulfed by sooty air. The fence railing had been bent as though it were a gob

of soft candy. Imperial tanks were overturned on the ground, and guns had been left abandoned by the retreating Imperial soldiers.

A single witch had brought upon this destruction.

"You wish to speak to me?"

Not a single member of the Imperial forces remained. In a blue expanse of sky so deep it felt like it could swallow her, there floated a tanned girl.

"What is it you want to talk about now, Crow?"

The Founder Nebulis.

As her dull golden hair fluttered in the wind, the greatest, oldest witch looked down at the ground. Below stood her younger brother, with whom she had fought and separated from.

Crossweil Gate Nebulis.

The original wielder of the astral swords had only one thing to say:

"A reflection."

"A *reflection*?"

"Nothing goes as planned… Yunmelngen and I have realized that—very keenly, too—for the past century." He let out a sigh. "I wonder when it was that I said this. *Yunmelngen and I haven't changed the Empire yet. But we found hope that we'll be able to.*"

"And?"

"Plenty of things happened in this land while you were asleep. Even after it burned down, the Empire revived. Actually, they didn't just rebuild it—they accelerated their advancement of technology. From your perspective, the capital might even look like a city from the future."

"And why do you think they did that?" His sister's words were like thorns. "Get to the point, Crow. The Empire has only

CHAPTER 2

developed because they fear witches, right? It's merely proof that they still view witches with hostility."

"You're right. I can't deny that."

He sighed again. He suddenly dropped his gaze from the sky.

"In the end, that was a miscalculation on my and Yunmelngen's part. Since the day the capital was reduced to ash, the Imperials have hated witches and sorcerers. And they've become afraid of them, too... That's why Yunmelngen and I stayed behind in the Empire and waited."

Time would heal all wounds. It would heal the deep-rooted fear of mages in the Empire. And the powerful hatred the Sovereignty felt toward the Imperial forces. Both would likely fade.

Even if it didn't happen in a decade or two, they had believed that perhaps things would change in fifty years, seventy, or maybe even a hundred.

"We realized later that this wouldn't turn out the way we expected."

He had repeated himself, not for his sister's sake, but for his own.

"The fighting between the Empire and the Sovereignty has increased day by day and started to lead to skirmishes worldwide. Instead of fading, the rage has been inherited by the next generations. I wasn't able to stop that from happening."

Their largest miscalculation had been Lord Yunmelngen's condition. After being possessed by the Planetary Calamity, like the Founder, the Lord had immediately gone into a slumber following their succession to the throne and woke only a few days a year.

"The only thing I could do was tell him what day it was when he woke and what had happened in the world while he slept. In the end, the Eight Great Apostles kept hold over their power, and the Imperial forces continued to expand."

The same had occurred in the Sovereignty. After the death of the first queen, Alicerose, the Nebulis bloodline had split into three families. The three royal families each had lands under their supervision and possessed astral corps, and they were stockpiling power in order to fight the Imperial forces.

"Crow." The Founder's voice was harsh. "That's not a reflection. It's a confession."

"..."

"I believe you told me before that you would stay in the Empire, and I had said, *Are you still obsessed with that dream?* It seems it took you a whole century to wake up."

Hmph. The sigh that left her mouth melted into the raging wind.

"Crow, you and Yunmelngen were mistaken from the start when you tried changing the Empire from within."

"I suppose that was the end result."

"Yes," she said. "So stay out of my way from now on."

The Empire was unchangeable. Lord Yunmelngen hadn't been able to change it in a century. The deep-rooted fear the Empire had of witches and sorcerers hadn't been something that could be dispelled so easily. As long as it remained, the persecution of astral mages would likely continue.

That was why…

"I will annihilate the Empire."

"That's no longer necessary."

Time stopped. They had both spoken at the same moment, and the tan girl floating in the sky had frozen, forgetting to even blink.

He hadn't agreed with her. The words he had uttered were so

CHAPTER 2

different from what she had expected that, for a moment, her brain had stopped functioning.

"……What?"

"I'm not done yet; in fact, it's the opposite. This is just the beginning."

Crossweil went on the move. The Founder needed only a glance to see that the sword in his left hand was nothing more than a copy of the real black astral sword.

"A replica?" she asked.

"That's right. I begged the Astrals to make it for me. The real ones are with Iska, after all."

"…"

Iska.

Crossweil couldn't help but notice that her brow furrowed upon hearing the boy's name.

"So I heard you fought against my idiot pupil."

"…What are you trying to say?"

"You were surprised, weren't you?"

"About what…?"

"In your eyes, what was he like?"

"Tsk." The girl floating in the air opened her eyes wide. For a moment, she stared into the ether as though she was trying to recall something, but then she came back to her senses and immediately pursed her lips.

"I don't remember him."

"You don't? I'm certain he was different from the other Imperial soldiers. For example—"

"Go back to sleep, Nebulis."
"Next time you wake up, I bet the world will be in a better place."

*　*　*

"Did he call you a witch?"

"＿＿"

"And why did he fight you? He didn't challenge you for revenge like the Imperial forces or others from the Empire, did he?"

"＿＿"

"I think not. And I'm pretty sure you realized why I entrusted the astral swords to him, too."

Crossweil had failed to change the Empire, and that was because he couldn't draw attention to himself as a sorcerer with astral powers.

He had realized the only one who could change the Empire was an Imperial. That was why he needed a successor.

"Yunmelngen and I couldn't do it, but he—"

"Croooow!"

The air trembled. The girl howled as loudly as she could, and the very sound of her voice had turned into a gigantic invisible shock wave that pushed everything away from her.

"…Crow…" She gritted her back teeth. "You couldn't possibly dare to try telling me the same thing you did back then… Even after I've come all this way…you wouldn't dare tell me to wait again. And all because you found a flimsy speck of hope in the Empire, a place that hasn't changed in any way for an entire century."

"That's exactly what I'm saying."

"Croooow!"

The Founder Nebulis's right hand sliced through the air. It was astral wind. The gust of wind blew the cars away like fallen leaves, then turned into a gigantic front of air that headed straight for Crossweil.

CHAPTER 2

* * *

He cut through the wind with his black blade.

"____"

With her arm still raised in the air, the Founder stopped as though she'd been frozen.

But she wasn't surprised. After all, she'd seen this happen in the past.

"So it's not purely for looks, then."

"No, it just seems like it has the same power, but it doesn't have the most important function the astral swords do."

Crossweil was expressionless as he held the black hilt of the sword. "This sword can't fight against the Planetary Calamity. Only the true astral swords can do that. I know I don't need to tell you that, but just to be clear," he said matter-of-factly.

He looked up at the sky, at his sister, who continued to float in the air.

"According to Yunmelngen, as your little brother, it's my duty to stop the world's most ferocious big sister."

At the farthest reaches of the Imperial territory, the two who had been siblings long ago clashed.

However…they had no way of knowing that at that moment, the Eight Great Apostles, the very ones who pulled the strings behind the Empire and Sovereignty, and the Imperial assembly itself were no more.

And…they had no way of knowing a true witch was starting her crusade to indiscriminately erase both the Empire's and Sovereignty's existence from the world in her merciless quest for world equality.

2

Empire, eighth checkpoint (northeast).

Had this been a time of peace, a line of a dozen private vehicles likely could have been spotted at the inspection area, but the checkpoint was as good as deserted.

The Grand Witch Nebulis had struck.

Because the Grand Witch had revived after a century of slumber and attacked the seventh checkpoint, all civilians had been evacuated from the area.

"Perfect. They made the right decision."

Clack...clack...

Along with the orderly echo of footsteps, a man in a mask sauntered right through the gate of the checkpoint.

"Now, if you'd like to know what is most wonderful about it, it's that they were perfectly correct in choosing to *leave* the Empire. From today, the Imperial territory will become a sea of flames. Instead of running through this checkpoint into the Empire, they fled to the neutral cities. What a wise decision."

The sound of a buzzer—the warning alarm—rang out. The moment the masked man had taken a single step through the gate, the sensor equipped at the checkpoint had begun to flash a bright red.

It was a large-scale astral-energy sensor. The masked man showed no sign of being disturbed by the clamor as he continued to walk through.

"And thanks to that, we are free to move as we like. It would be most irritating to have civilians making a fuss during our skirmish with the Imperial forces, after all."

A dozen or so men and women followed after him. Though they were disguised as suit-wearing civilians, as they passed by, the astral-energy detectors continued to blare. The alarm was shrill and strikingly loud as it howled.

"I apologize for keeping you waiting, dear Uncle."

A girl wearing a blindfold gracefully walked toward him. She was likely thirteen, maybe fourteen. Her long black hair had a beautiful sheen, and her dress was gorgeous and ornate. Though her eyes were covered, her delicate nose and mouth made her look as charming as a doll.

The buzzer began to sound even louder. The alarm made it clear this girl possessed more astral energy than the masked man and his subordinates combined.

"I had lunch," she said.

"That was very quick, Kissing. You could have taken your time, you know."

Uncle.

Lord Mask turned to the black-haired girl, Kissing.

"We need a break as it is. It will take some time for Shanorotte to meet us here, and we will not be able to invade the Imperial capital as confidently without her guidance."

"Will we meet her here?"

Kissing looked slightly hesitant, which was highly unusual for her. It seemed she had reservations about what her uncle—the dearest person in the world to her—had just told her.

"____"

"What is it, Kissing? If you have something on your mind, do speak up."

"It's too noisy here."

"Ah yes, I suppose you are right. You can turn off the sensor, and the gate as well… Hmm? How odd." Lord Mask placed a hand on his chin and pondered something. Kissing looked up at him in curiosity. "We have activated the alarms, after all. I would expect

CHAPTER 2

the Imperial soldiers to come rushing in… Did they really evacuate every single person from the checkpoint?"

The Imperial forces had yet to show hide or hair of themselves. Considering the clamor the alarm was making, the Imperial soldiers on guard should have naturally come running, but not a single one had appeared.

"Our Revered Founder is attacking the checkpoint next to this one. I could understand if they sent over reinforcements, but it seems rather foolish to leave this place entirely unguarded."

The Founder was currently attacking the seventh checkpoint. Because of that, the Nebulis Sovereignty had sent assassins to another location in order to infiltrate the Empire while she created an opening. It was an old trick that the Imperial forces should have been able to anticipate.

"And this is still the border, after all. There should be at least one or two soldiers here to communicate with the rest of the forces. What in the world are the Imperials thinking?"

He headed toward the inspection area with his subordinates and Kissing walking behind him. The alarm continued to wail, trying to warn others of an unprecedented number of astral-corps members attempting to invade the location.

It continued for seconds…then minutes…

Regardless of how long they waited, not a single soldier showed any sign of storming in.

Why?

Then their malaise grew, turning into full-blown suspicion.

"Are those people?"

The moment one of the subordinates said this, they noticed a pile of bodies scattered around the inspection area. The closer they approached, the more striking the scene became. And there, Lord Mask saw something most peculiar indeed.

"What in the world is this?!"

They were Imperial soldiers who were still holding on to their guns. Some still sat in the driver's seat of their vehicles, but not a single one so much as moved or opened their eyes.

The entire force had been decimated.

What could it mean?

Just what had happened?

"What is this...?" Even Kissing expressed her confusion.

They had been prepared to fight the Imperial forces once they arrived, yet someone else had come before them and annihilated their hundred-year-old enemy. And of all places, they'd defeated the soldiers at the border.

"Uncle, what do you think happened?"

"You wait here, Kissing, though I doubt they're pretending to have fallen." Lord Mask wandered alone into the space.

He observed them. The strangest thing he noticed was that not a single soldier seemed to have any external wounds. Then what had done this to them?

"It doesn't seem to be poison gas. My, my..."

Thump.

He kicked a soldier's head. They did not react. However, he noticed the slightest, nearly imperceptible movement of the soldier's chest as it rose and fell. He could also just barely hear the soldier breathe as well.

"So they're alive... Which means they're sleeping...or rather they've been knocked unconscious? But this is still strange, nonetheless. Especially as the alarm is making such a clamor, and they show no sign of waking."

Something felt off. In fact, it went beyond that—it felt ominous.

CHAPTER 2

He knew of astral powers that could hypnotize, but the Imperial forces were the very people who would be the most likely to dedicate themselves to finding countermeasures to such attacks.

Yet those very people had been wiped out?

And not even one had been hurt in the process. All of them were fast asleep. This seemed incredibly unrealistic. He had never seen such a tranquil method of defeating soldiers before.

"This is truly odd. Someone dealt with the Imperial forces before us? But it looks as though they never fought, which means…"

He couldn't come up with scenarios that would have resulted in this. Even as the proxy leader of the Zoa, one of the royal families, Lord Mask couldn't think of any method that could incapacitate the Imperial forces in such a manner.

And that irritated him.

"Come, Kissing. It seems we can approach this area, but make sure not to accidentally touch them."

"Yes, dearest Uncle."

The girl gracefully walked toward him; however, she stopped right before she entered the area.

"…"

"What is it, Kissing?"

"……No."

"Hmm?"

"Nooo! Ahhh!"

Her scream could no longer form intelligible words. In front of Lord Mask and the subordinates, the girl began to suddenly spasm as she held her head and screamed. The blindfold she wore fluttered down to reveal her eyes, which glowed purple.

Kissing Zoa Nebulis IX had a great gift.

Her astral crest appeared within her eyes. All astral mages had crests that would appear on their bodies. However, never in history had anyone had a crest in their eyes except Kissing. She could see astral energy.

Kissing visualized astral energy with tens of thousands—even a million—times greater precision than any Imperial cutting-edge sensor.

Because of that, Kissing was a secret weapon. She was the Zoa family's weapon for their scheme to fight against astral mages.

"No…! Don't…don't come near me!"

And now that very girl was screaming.

She had seen something. Right at that moment, in that space, she had seen a monster the likes of which she had never seen before drawing near.

"Kissing? Calm down. What in the world do you see—?"

"Oh, I thought I recognized you."

A flirtatious voice echoed around them.

Right in front of Lord Mask and the others, a black current began pouring out from a crack in the paved road—a black vortex.

That was all it could be described as. The black current spiraled into the air and condensed into a humanoid silhouette. It turned into a pitch-black monster without eyes or a mouth.

Thump…

It was as though their hearts were being squeezed. Cold sweat began to drip from Lord Mask's brow.

"What?!"

Immediately, he grabbed Kissing and pushed her behind him. With just one look, he understood the Imperial forces had been annihilated by this monster—and it was also what Kissing had seen.

"_____"

CHAPTER 2

The monster stared at him but suddenly turned away to face the fallen soldiers.

"Are you worried about them, Lord Mask? They were so rude. **They called me a monster and began to attack me. So I decided to punish them a bit.**"

"Wha—?!" He was so surprised, his voice cracked. How did this monster know his name?

"Now, what do we have here…?" He hid Kissing, who continued to shiver, behind him and took a step forward. He was in front of his subordinates, after all. If he, their leader, flinched, it would affect his troops' morale. "Why would such a grotesque being know my name?"

"**How uncalled for,**" the thing said dramatically as it placed a hand on its cheek and feigned being hurt. "**Did you forget who I am, Lord Mask? But we had such an exhilarating tryst in the Moon Spire.**"

"What?!"

"**Oh, I kid.**" The monster's voice returned to its usual tone without skipping a beat. It laughed like a devil. "**My voice echoes so much in this form that it seems humans have trouble hearing me. But what a disappointment to see even you can't recognize me.**"

It traced a fingertip over its large bosom. Had the monster been human, its curves most certainly would have been described as *captivating*. And its voice had taken on a bewitching tone.

"…" There was only one person who came to mind. "Elletear… is that you?"

"**What an honor it is that you realized.**"

His subordinates began to murmur. Of course they wouldn't be able to hold back their shock. The greatest beauty of the palace—no, the greatest beauty in the Sovereignty—and this black mist-like monster were nothing alike. It was as though she were a shadow of herself.

"Then did you do this to the Imperial forces?"

"**It was such an enjoyable endeavor.**" The monster that claimed to be Elletear opened her arms wide. "**I showed what is supposedly the largest military force in the world a little love, and they helplessly fell right over. How very, very adorable they are.**"

"Oh...?" Lord Mask's impression of the situation changed with that response. Learning how the first princess of the Lou family had ended up like this, what power she had used on the Imperial forces—those were things to figure out later. Understanding what had happened would take time. The most appropriate action now would be to determine how he could use her and her power to defang the Imperial forces. With the Founder and Elletear, they would be able to take down the Imperial capital in a single night.

"Shall we escort you, then?" He echoed Elletear's actions and opened his own arms. "You are a fellow astral mage. Come with us, my dear Elletear. This is the most perfect time to destroy the Empire with our Revered Founder."

"**Yes, we do not need the Empire. As far as I am concerned, it can disappear.**"

"Wonderful. In that case—"

"**Just like the Sovereignty.**"

She laughed.

For a moment, Lord Mask wasn't able to understand the meaning behind her enchanting smile, and he simply stood there.

"What did you say...?"

"**I no longer need the Sovereignty, the Revered Founder, or any member of the royal family at all! You're no use to me.**"

CHAPTER 2

"What are you saying, my dear Elletear?" His voice grew hoarse, and his throat went dry. "You're a Sovereign princess. You're the queen's own beloved daughter, aren't you?"
"I am a witch."
"?"
"I've always wanted to become one. The world's final witch. The true witch. A being who neither the Empire nor the Sovereignty can stop."
The monster once again placed a hand on her breast.
"Who cares about the Founder or purebred types? A country ruled only by the select astral mages from the royal family isn't a paradise. So I will destroy it. I will destroy the Zoa, Hydra, and Lou, and I will create a true paradise."
"..."
"Rejoice, Lord Mask. The Zoa family's most cherished wish to destroy the Empire comes true today. So please worry not as you fall as well."
"Wait... I don't understand what you mean by all this, but..." Under his mask, his eyes were as sharp as a hawk's. "I suppose this means the thing in front of me isn't Elletear—you're simply a monster!"
"I'm glad to see you're quick on the uptake." The monster of darkness's voice was jubilant with delight. "**Even I was hesitant to harm a person who wouldn't resist. So please, go ahead and use your power against me. The royal family's power, a purebred's power.**"
However...
She said briefly between her words, "**It will be in vain.**"
Clang!
A knife had pierced the road. It had gone right through Elletear's transformed body and embedded itself in the ground behind her.

"Oh?"

"My, Lord Mask, how frightening. You would throw a knife at someone without warning?"

Elletear placed her hands around her own throat where the knife had traveled through. Had she been human, blood would have been spurting out, but the knife hadn't so much as harmed her. It had simply passed through her like a blade going through water or air. It was most likely the same for the Imperial forces' bullets and cannon fire.

"I do wonder what trick is behind that. Behind your body."

"It isn't a body at all. Right now, I am something like a crystallization of astral energy."

"So you're astral power!"

"No, something more frightening than that."

The true witch stretched out her hand to him. The subordinates behind Lord Mask readied themselves. They would not let her approach. Elletear's, or the monster that she had become, power still remained a mystery, and given that she had taken down the Imperial forces, their best option was to stop her before she could use it again.

"This is an excuse I was not even looking to find..."

"What we are eradicating is a monster. She is not a Lou princess!"

They were the Zoa family's elite troops. Fire, lightning, frost, and shock waves came from all directions and swallowed the monster in the blink of an eye. She had nowhere to run.

The dozens of astral powers collided and burst in a chain reaction; then, as the wind rushed out after the impact, it whipped through the entire checkpoint. The energy had condensed, and as it crystallized, light was released.

That was how powerful the barrage had been. Considering

that, the epicenter of the maelstrom shouldn't have allowed any physical material to remain intact...

"**Oh, what a beautiful sound.**"

Yet they heard her croon out. In the center of the crater that had been dug from the road, they found a monster gazing at the blue sky as though she was simply pensive about something or other. There was not a scratch on her.

"**You all were born with powerful abilities. And the chorus your powers produce as they layer upon one another creates such a vigorous tone. I never had that. No matter how I wished for it, I was simply never born with that power. I do admire you, however...**"

You are all fools.

"Uh?!"

"But we hit her! She's unscathed?!"

The Zoa's elite forces grimaced. They hadn't defeated her at all. Instead of feeling pain, the monster had perceived their attacks as only a comforting "sound."

"**Now, all of you, of the Zoa household.**" She spoke from deep within the crater.

Elletear—the monster—made her way up the slope. She took each step one at a time, walking slowly as though she enjoyed watching the astral corps standing outside the crater shudder in fear.

"**Because you were blessed with powerful abilities from birth, you were treasured and praised before you were even aware of your surroundings. Because you led such brilliant, dazzling lives, you likely became conceited enough to believe you were the chosen ones. And that is what upsets me.**"

It wasn't like that for Elletear Lou Nebulis IX.

Her astral power had been too weak. Due to that single flaw, Elletear had been deemed a failure from birth. She wasn't qualified to become queen. In the palace and in the Sovereignty, no one had sworn their allegiance to her. There was no value in a princess who had no promise of becoming queen.

She had always been alone.

"The Zoa, Hydra, and Lou are the same. You all thought you brought glory to the Sovereignty and were protectors of the astral mages' paradise. But you are gravely mistaken."

The Founder's bloodline had become too proud.

If the Sovereignty were truly a paradise for all astral mages, why was someone such as Elletear cast aside as useless, as a failure of the royal family?

The weak astral mages had been rejected by the Empire, and the Sovereignty scorned them for being useless, so where were they meant to go to find their place?

"I will build it. I will build a true, loving paradise for the astral mages that is neither the Empire nor the Sovereignty."

"In that form?" He sneered. The leader of the Zoa, Lord Mask, squeezed the black-haired girl's right hand. "A human should serve humans. It would have been one thing if you were still a princess, but now no one would be drawn to a monster like you. Come now, Kissing."

"…Uh!" Kissing Zoa Nebulis lifted her face. Her strange eyes that held her astral crest glared at the genuine witch standing before her.

"I…find you…frightening…but still…"

"Well, Ms. Kissing, it seems you've finally become capable of speaking for yourself. You seem much more mature than when I first met you."

"Do not listen to the witch. I am with you."

"Yes, dearest Uncle!" the purebred Kissing Zoa Nebulis howled. She threw out her hands toward the sky with such force that her dress fluttered about. "Disappear, you monster!"

March of thorns—the Whole of Creation.

The air trembled. Enough black thorns to blot out the sky had appeared at the checkpoint.

She had created tens of thousands of thorns made from astral power. If they all rained down on the checkpoint, the entire establishment would likely disappear. The thorns surrounded Elletear from all sides and pierced her at once.

"Ugh!"

The monster shrieked... But a moment later, even the scream disappeared under the thorns as though nothing had existed there in the first place.

"I-it's gone?"

"Lady Kissing made it disappear with her thorns...?"

The subordinates stood there in stunned silence. In front of them, Lord Mask lovingly tousled the girl's hair.

"Good job, Kissing. That was surprisingly easier than anticipated. It seems even after turning into a monster, she was powerless when erased from existence."

"...Y-yes, dearest Uncle." Kissing's shoulders heaved as she attempted to breathe. That had been the largest and fastest attack she had made against anyone. She had no idea how the monster would react, so to prevent it from evading her or blocking her, she had used her full abilities.

"D-did it truly work...?" she asked.

"Yes, indeed. Just look. That terrible monster is gone... Ah yes. I truly did not wish for Elletear to meet an end like this. But allowing her to sleep forevermore is a mercy compared to letting her live as that monster."

The subordinates began to clap quietly. It wasn't clear whether they were applauding Kissing's victory or sending off the princess who had turned into a monster.

"That battle left a rather terrible aftertaste. Now then…" Lord Mask lifted his hand. The applause stopped. The subordinates had understood what he meant, but there was one person who continued to clap.

"That's enough."

Clap, clap.

"I said that's enough. Who is doing that?" Lord Mask turned around, but he found his people were not clapping. "Huh?!"

No one was clapping at all.

But he could clearly hear the applause continuing.

"It can't be…?!"

"How terrible of you, Kissing. That was so very painful."

Black light began to burble up from thin air. The dark current swirled until it condensed into the form of a person.

"…Impossible."

Lord Mask felt a drop of cold sweat trickle down his cheek. Though his calm demeanor had not wavered even in front of the revived Founder, he was now consumed by an unprecedented fear. The black-haired girl beside him felt the same.

"Uh…n…no…"

"Oh, I'm so sorry, Kissing. Don't look at me with such eyes full of fear. I'm still not used to others looking at me like that; it pains me."

She laughed. Though her words were apologetic, she sounded positively gleeful.

"Then again, I suppose a witch is a terrifying thing, so it is fitting for how I am now."

There was a faint glow around the throat of the dark, transparent monster. That was where Elletear's astral crest had appeared when she was human.

"My astral power is Voice. All my power could do was mimic another person's voice. I couldn't use it in battle or for political gain. It was a useless ability with entertainment value at most."

The monster dramatically turned to the heavens like an opera singer taking the stage.

"Now that I have this power and am in this form, both my astral power and I have been reborn. And my power has become the astral power of the planet's song—one that sings of the end."

Her Voice power had transformed into the Song astral power.

She was the divine star mutant. Whatever calamity had transformed Princess Elletear had also mutated her astral power.

"Listen to the world's last witch and the blight of her song."

And so the true witch sang. She sang the curse of calamity that would transform the very world.

"I will let you listen to the requiem of the planet."

CHAPTER 3

Archenemy

1

More than five thousand meters underground, the Imperial capital.

A hundred years ago, the excavation site once known as the Planet's Navel had become the present-day location of the Imperial assembly, where the supreme authority pulling the strings behind the Empire existed.

After taking a step off the elevator, one would be greeted by the solemn sight of several hundred seats set up in the hall. Naturally, everyone, including Iska, had expected to be greeted by such a sight as well.

But it was empty.

The ceiling had collapsed.

There was a gigantic hole inside the hall like someone had fired a rocket cannon, and the Eight Great Apostles' monitors had been left strewn across the ground, mercilessly shattered to pieces. But the most surprising was…

"Eek?!"

The moment Sisbell saw it, her voice cracked. The hall was in such disarray that Mismis and Nene standing next to Iska gasped in surprise, and even Jhin narrowed his eyes in bewilderment from behind.

"Hey… Is this some kind of joke?" Jhin clucked his tongue as he looked at the walls. Among the scattered debris was a silver mechanical soldier that barely retained its original form. "Iska, that huge thing, it's…"

"I think it's an astralnomical soldier. It looks the same as the one Luclezeus used."

There had been another one.

However, this one had been destroyed to the point that it was almost unrecognizable.

Had it been crushed by the falling ceiling? No, that couldn't have caused this. The machine had been mercilessly decimated. There was also one other thing that was concerning.

"Where are they…?"

Iska looked over the vestiges of the hall. The only light source was the feeble illumination of the elevator. When she noticed Iska scrutinizing the scene, Sisbell approached him out of curiosity.

"Iska? What have you been looking for?"

"The Eight Great Apostles."

"What?"

"All their monitors have been smashed. There isn't a single one left. The astralnomical soldier has been completely destroyed, and the assembly hall is in ruins…"

CHAPTER 3

He broke out into a cold sweat.
It couldn't be…
Iska could think of only one possibility, but could it even be?

The Eight Great Apostles had been defeated.

They must have fought against something in the assembly hall. That was what he could gather based on the astralnomical soldier, but he couldn't imagine what sort of power could have caused this destruction—at least not easily.

"So even the Eight Great Apostles couldn't stand a chance…," he heard someone whisper. Risya seemed to have been talking to herself, but it echoed through the quiet hall. "What a monster they've created. Based on this, it looks like they've gotten pretty far into completing their work. What should we do, Your Excellency?"

"**That's exactly why we're here to investigate.**"

The silvery beastperson turned to the girl with strawberry-blond hair and urged her, "**Come, Princess Sisbell. I have one more job to request of you.**"

2

Imperial territory, seventh checkpoint.

Now that Alice thought about it, she should have believed it. She should have realized that the imminent calamity she had sensed from the dark clouds covering the sky the night before was real.

"Lady Alice, we have received a report from the scouting unit. They say the Founder was floating in the air above the seventh checkpoint but disappeared…!"

"Huh? But we followed her all this way!"

The checkpoint...

The moment they caught sight of the gate, Shuvalts, the elderly attendant in the driver's seat, had yelled as he held the comm against his ear. "It seems the seventh checkpoint is empty. The civilians and even the Imperial forces have already evacuated the area. What would you like to do?"

"Continue straight in." She leaned forward from the back seat. "I'm sure the Founder is headed to the Imperial capital. It'll be convenient for us if no one is around up ahead. We'll be able to pass right through into the Empire then."

"Yes, but it'll take a full day to arrive at the Imperial capital from here."

"...I'm well aware."

She clenched her fists on top of her thighs.

After flying on a plane, taking a train, and speeding down the highway, they had finally made it to the Empire. The very checkpoint where the Founder had appeared was right before her eyes, but the Founder was out of her grasp.

...... *I failed to catch her.*

...... *If I'd just been half an hour faster, I could have caught her at the checkpoint.*

However, she didn't have time to lament that now.

"Shuvalts! Get in touch with the operatives in the Empire. Have them leave the Imperial capital immediately. Tell them they will be in danger once the Founder appears."

"Yes, Lady Alice. But I'm afraid there will be a slight delay..."

"What?"

"Hmm... Understood," the elderly attendant said into the comm. "I have received another report. It seems there is an eighth

CHAPTER 3

checkpoint after the seventh. They believe the Zoa have passed through it."

"Yes. And I believe another unit is following them."

"They have lost communication."

"What does that mean? They lost sight of the Zoa?"

"…No." The attendant heavily shook his head. "Our forces at the eighth checkpoint stopped responding several minutes ago. We can only hope it is a device malfunction…"

"You think the Zoa noticed them?"

"There is a possibility that the Founder teleported to the eighth checkpoint when she disappeared from the seventh. Perhaps she plans to destroy the entire border before moving on to the capital?"

"——" Alice had a bad feeling about this. At that moment, she recalled the sense of foreboding she'd felt the night before.

"Change of plans, Shuvalts. The eighth checkpoint is in the vicinity, isn't it? Head there posthaste!"

"As you wish."

He turned left toward the eighth checkpoint where they had lost contact with their unit.

However, what Alice saw was a deserted area.

"What?!"

She doubted her very eyes. She could understand why there would be no civilians around, as they likely would have run in fear from the Founder's attack, but where had the Imperial forces gone?

They had even left the iron gate open. None of the soldiers acting as guards were there. Only the astral-energy alarm was blaring.

"Shuvalts, stay here. Please handle all correspondence."

She left him in the car and dashed out to the checkpoint on her own. But it was strange. Despite having headed further in, she still saw no signs of a battle.

……The Zoa did pass through here, didn't they?
……If Lord Mask and Kissing were here, I would imagine they would have fought against the Imperial forces.

But she saw no signs of that.

If the Imperial soldiers and the Zoa's elite forces had clashed, she should have seen bullets strewn everywhere as well as marks left from astral powers. She began to feel suspicious along with a growing sense of unease, then all her emotions exploded when she saw the dozens of victims in front of her on the ground.

Both the Imperial forces and the astral corps had been annihilated.

The soldiers had collapsed while still holding their guns, and the astral mages had fallen with their hands outstretched as though they were in the middle of using their powers. There had been no distinction made between who was an Imperial or who was part of the Sovereignty.

Every last person had been mercilessly taken down.

"Lord Mask?"

Among the many fallen, she spotted one particular man. It was the Zoa's proxy leader.

"Lord Mask? Please wake up! What in the world…?!"

She found no external wounds. However, he didn't respond to his name or to her slapping his face. Was he in a coma? Or had he been severely weakened?

"Even Lord Mask is in this state… This can't be true…"

The situation was nothing short of bizarre. None of the Imperial forces or the other astral mages were hurt, either. It was almost as though they had been wiped out by a dream they couldn't wake from.

CHAPTER 3

This couldn't have been the Founder's doing. It was exactly the opposite of the mass destruction she would have caused.

"Oh, I wondered who could have arrived."

Alice shuddered.

She had heard a voice from behind her, even though she was sure nothing should have been there. Alice leaped and whirled around as though a lump of ice had been pressed against her neck. And there, in that very space…

…she found a dark, transparent monster in the shape of a human standing there.

"Eek?!" Her throat tightened as she let out a garbled scream.

What was it? What was the monster that had just appeared before her?

"Why, if it isn't Alice. So even you've come to the Empire, then. Did you come to save Sisbell?"

"…What?"

"Oh, how mean of you. Did you really have to scream upon seeing me?"

The monster placed a hand against its cheek. It smiled elegantly like a woman as it spoke to her.

But how did the monster know her name? And why did it sound so familiar? Though she found it difficult to hear because its voice echoed, there was something graceful and quiet about its tone. It was almost as though it felt nostalgic.

"…No… It can't be…"

When she thought about it, she did know someone who had become something similar.

The witch Vichyssoise.

Iska had claimed the girl from the house of Hydra had turned into a monster and attacked him. And the person Alice thought of now was…

"Sis…ter?"

"Hee-hee. Bull's-eye."

The monster transformed. The darkness began to regain color, turning into a beautiful goddess's form. Her fluttering emerald hair was tinged with gold, and her features were well defined and beautiful. Her large bosom seemed close to spilling out of the black wedding dress she wore.

"…"

It was her very own sister.

Alice was speechless when she figured out the identity of the monster. She felt the blood drain from her face. If she had a mirror, Alice could imagine her lips would be blue. In contrast…

"So, Alice."

Her sister's eyes were eerily tender.

"I think it's rather funny. If I were in their place, I'd run immediately, but they didn't."

Alice turned around. In front of her were the fallen Imperial forces and astral corps.

Lord Mask was also among them.

"They probably realized they couldn't win against me, but they just had no idea what that meant. Both the Imperial forces and the astral corps have always been in a position of power, so they've never felt the experience of being hunted before. That's why not even one of them ran."

Every single one of them was down on the ground, and not a single one had regained consciousness.

"How disappointing. They remained satisfied with the weapons and astral powers bestowed upon them and ended up being so frail."

"Did you do this? Did you do that to them?"

CHAPTER 3

Elletear grinned. It was a broad smile.

"Well, they're nothing but nuisances."

"Wha—!"

Just that single phrase shattered Alice's entire image of Elletear of seventeen years. The one in front of her was her sister—however, she realized the sister she had known all this time had truly been a monster at heart.

"Sister..." Her trembling lips desperately formed words. "What are you trying to achieve...? How could you call our family *nuisances*? I understand the Imperial forces, but how could you do this to Lord Mask...?"

"So, Alice," her sister replied, her eyes still tender. "Those who have astral powers have come to be called astral mages. And they are the ones feared by the Empire. The Nebulis Sovereignty offered the mages a helping hand, and that was why it was lauded as a paradise for all mages."

"Sister? What are you trying to say...?"

"Those were all lies." The smile reached her sister's eyes, but it was not one of affection. It was a sneer for a hopeless fool. "The Nebulis Sovereignty is a country where astral powers reign supreme. Those with the best astral powers rise while others are not even allowed to try. The fact that they are considered extraordinary makes them even worse than the Empire."

"What?! What are you trying to say?!" Alice yelled as loudly as she could, her lips pale. "Y-yes, I suppose that is one aspect of the Sovereignty, but strong astral mages are only treasured because they defend the country. If we didn't do that, we couldn't resist the Empire..."

"And is that true for the queen as well?"

"Of course! If she wasn't powerful, she wouldn't be a match for any of the Empire's assassins!"

There was a firm reason for it, and a reason for why the conclave that had been upheld for a century selected powerful queens.

"Even Mother has said so. The role of the queen is to make the people feel safe. Though that isn't her only duty, it is one reason why the queen must have strong powers!"

"In order to resist the Empire?"

"That's right!"

"Then what about *after* the Empire is defeated?"

"......Huh?"

"Alice, your claim is correct. At the very least, it was something established for a great cause—only until the Empire was defeated." Her sister eyed her. "Then what happens *after* the Empire is defeated? Would it become a country that could recognize the worth of weak mages like myself?"

"I—I..."

"It wouldn't." A long sigh escaped her sister's lips. She showed a deep, deep sense of resignation, as though she found hopelessness in everything in the world. "Isn't it true? If the Sovereignty did defeat the Empire, it would be thanks to the powerful mages. Those who are powerful would become lionized even more in the era that's ushered in. And the weak mages would have even less of a role."

"......"

"Do you understand now? In fact, if the Empire was defeated, I think that would only serve to accelerate astral-power supremacy in the Nebulis Sovereignty. Those born with strong astral powers would use them to crush the Empire, and the powerful queen would be hailed as well. Nothing would change."

"B-but, Sister...!"

"So I made a decision." She placed a hand on her large bosom.

"I'll destroy both the Empire and the Sovereignty."

CHAPTER 3

*　*　*

That single statement left Alice speechless. "Sister..."

"There are many other weak mages like myself. I'll create a true paradise that accepts them as well. But that won't be possible with someone as powerful as you around... No... In fact, you're nothing but an obstacle. I'd almost rather you disappear."

"Huh?"

"Perhaps I'll do the same to you as I did to Lord Mask."

Alice had realized it too late—her sister's calm smile was like that of a predator eyeing its prey. Her sister had no qualms about killing her.

Alice immediately went on guard.

"Oh, but never mind!" The whole thing was so sudden. Her older sister abruptly shrugged, as though it was a joke. "You are my dear little sister, after all."

"......Huh?"

"I'd like to just pluck you gently, like a wildflower. But you are strong, so you'd put up quite a fight, which would mean trouble for me. As I am now, I think I wouldn't be able to control my power, and I would crush you."

"Sister!"

In that moment, all her fear disappeared. She was being looked down upon. The humiliation made her feel hot, as though all the blood in her body had begun to boil. "Be reasonable! I won't hold back after you've been so hostile toward me, even if you are my sister!"

"So, Alice." Alice had shouted loudly enough to make her voice hurt, but her sister's voice remained matter-of-fact. "Do you have a knight who would protect you?"

"?"

"You've reached your limit. See, you're at it even now." Her sister pointed at her—at Alice, who stood alone. "You've always fought on your own. And you've made it through that way, but now you're facing something much more powerful than yourself."

"I… You don't know that for sure, not until we fight!"

"That's not what I meant." Her sister shook her head. "This is a story between a witch and a knight."

"What are you…?"

She didn't understand. She had no idea what her sister meant. A knight? Why was she talking about something so old-fashioned? This was the time of armies, personal soldiers, and convoys. Alice was confused by the old-fashioned word that seemed like it had come straight from another century.

Was she trying to confuse Alice on purpose? Alice was wary, simply because of her sister's bizarre choice of words. However…

"Hee-hee. I suppose you're too young for this. It's an adult matter, after all." Her sister seemed worked up. Her face glowed red, as though she couldn't hide her excitement, and she bashfully placed a hand on her cheek. "I needed one because I was so weak."

"……?"

"Because witches are so weak, they can't fight without a knight to protect them. Yes. No matter what era it is, a knight always seems to protect a princess."

"Sister?"

"Alice, astral power isn't as omnipotent as you believe. Astral powers are so frightened of me that your self-defenses have hesitated. You see?"

"What?"

"Joheim, please go easy on her."

Alice hadn't felt anyone else's presence, but once she noticed the person who had silently snuck up on her, she turned around in that moment in a panic.

CHAPTER 3

Shoom.

She felt a sharp pain in her side. She had been hit by the handle of a sword. When she realized it, the pain spread to the rest of her internal organs, and she nearly lost consciousness, almost falling to the ground.

"Huh? …Gah…ah…?"

The pain was so intense, she could hardly breathe. She felt dizzy, an intense nausea coming over her. She couldn't look up and fell to her knees.

"Wh-who…?!"

Her eyes opened wide. As Alice coughed, she looked up as her vision blurred.

She saw a red-haired Imperial soldier holding a sword.

The Saint Disciple of the first feat, the "Flash" Knight Joheim.

She couldn't have mistaken him for anyone else. He was the villain who had attacked the Queen's Palace and cut her mother. He was also the man who had hurt Elletear, but Alice realized that had been nothing more than one of her sister's other plans.

…… *That's right. So that was it.*

…… *It was my sister who called the Imperial forces in as well.*

That had been the turning point that caused the Sovereignty's upheaval. Because her mother, the queen, had been attacked by this man and forced to rest, her centralizing power had been lost. That had been the deciding factor that caused the full schism among the three royal families.

It was simply unforgivable. If only this man had never existed.

"Uh…guh…!"

"You see? Witches are weak." Her sister smiled faintly; then she turned her back on Alice and walked over to Joheim. "This is the difference between the two of us. I have a knight by my side. Alice, do you have a knight who will fight beside you?"

"...Huh?"

"You don't. You were too strong, so you fought alone. That's why you don't have one, and why you cannot win against me."

"Sis...ter...!"

"And I think I've changed my mind. I can't stand to see you in such pain." The witch blushed. "Alice, I think I would like you to disappear right here and now."

3

Five thousand meters underground.

In the cavern the Imperial assembly had existed in just a mere hour before.

"Good-bye, criminals of the past."

"Both the Planet's Navel and the Imperial assembly, the very symbol of authority—you've always wanted to go down together, haven't you?"

The rubble had fallen. The monitors the Eight Great Apostles possessed had been destroyed.

That had all been reproduced.

"Haah... Uh... H-how many times do you plan to abuse my power? I've reached my limit!" Sisbell sat down, having become exhausted. Her Illumination astral crest on her chest steadily lost its light. "Trying to use Illumination for long periods of time is like...haah...ah...trying to hold my breath. I really do have a limit!"

She was panting and desperately trying to regain her breath.

CHAPTER 3

As Iska and the others watched, the third princess of the Sovereignty took on a serious expression.

"Oh, Elletear…" Her voice was so faint, it seemed close to disappearing. She couldn't help but let out a sob, and her thoughts seemed to be in disarray from the shock of the reality she couldn't accept.

The witch Elletear.

In the scene her Illumination had re-created, the moment that the princess with goddess-like looks had turned into a monster, Iska hadn't been able to hold back his discomposure, so of course Sisbell would feel shocked, considering they shared the same blood.

"There was another one before this, too, wasn't there?" Jhin muttered.

"Vichyssoise from the Hydra family, wasn't it? She also turned into some monster and attacked us, didn't she? Is Elletear the same as that?"

"Oh, Jhin-Jhin, now, that's a dangerous way to think of this."

"……What?"

"You're right that they're similar, but only in the sense that they both ended up like that from Kelvina's experiments under the Eight Great Apostles' orders. But Elletear should never have been created." Risya pushed up her glasses. Behind the lenses, her eyes were bright and sharp as needles. "The Eight Great Apostles weren't able to control her. So what shall we do, Your Excellency? It looks like holding that thing back will be very difficult. "

"Agh… I hope you genuinely regret what you did, Apostles." The beastperson sighed in resignation. **"So they made a monster even they couldn't control, then exited the stage. Oh well… I think we need to go after her before she evolves. Well, there we have it, Black Steel's Successor."**

"Huh?"

He noticed the Lord turn their head slightly as though to look at the astral swords. Iska gulped.

"Are you saying *I* should stop her?"

"That thing is no longer Elletear or the princess anymore. If we leave her to do as she pleases, both the Empire and the Sovereignty are done for. At least, she'll evolve until she becomes a monster that will be able to accomplish that."

"W-wait!" yelled Sisbell, who was still sitting on the ground. She borrowed Rin's hand to stand up. "So you're going to stop my sister…?"

"That isn't your sister anymore. She's a witch who will destroy the world."

"She's my sister!" Sisbell glared at the Lord and bit her lip. "No matter how she changes, she's still my sister. Please let me talk to her."

"Talk? I think you'll only find tragic results if you do that."

"Even so, I'll still go to her!"

"All right," the Lord said.

"……Huh? Are you sure?"

"I doubt the witch has any emotions left in her, but in the 0.01 percent possibility you can convince her to stop, we might as well give it a try. But if it doesn't work, I'm not the one who'll suffer. It'll be you, Princess Sisbell. And you should be prepared for that."

Lord Yunmelngen snapped their fingers.

"Planet's Defense, Phage."

It was bright white—like paint was blotting everything out—as walls appeared and wriggled in midair, surrounding Iska and the others.

"Yeek!"

"Wh-what are these gross things?! Why are the walls moving?!"

CHAPTER 3

Nene leaped back, and Commander Mismis turned pale. Behind them, Rin grabbed Sisbell and yelled, "Watch out!" Lord Yunmelngen glanced at them, seeing their various reactions.

"The type of astral power that took to me a hundred years ago was the kind that burdens me with the Planet's Defense. In human terms, it's something like an immune system's white blood cells. Unfortunately, it'll only listen to me when I'm doing something that protects the planet." The Lord waved their arms around like a conductor. **"Do you hear me, astral powers? We're going to fight that witch, so follow her scent and take us to her."**

—Is io miel.—May it be done.—

He couldn't tell whether it was male or female, a child's or an adult's, but a neutral voice surrounded him from the walls all around; then his vision wavered for a moment. He felt as though his consciousness was fading, as though he was suddenly drowsy.

The eighth checkpoint.

When he came to his senses, the grounds of the inspection area sprawled in front of him, surrounded by metal fencing.

"We're at the border?! If we've been brought all the way here, then my sister Elletear must also be here!"

"So we got blasted off from the Imperial capital to the border a few hundred kilometers away. That's a pretty extravagant power."

Sisbell looked around while Rin seemed taken aback next to her.

However…Rin almost immediately scowled.

An alarm began ringing. She had gotten caught by the astral-energy detectors—at least, she'd likely gone on guard assuming that that was what had happened.

"What is the meaning of this?" Rin narrowed her eyes with suspicion. "Why aren't there any Imperial soldiers coming even though the alarms are going off? Hey, Imperial swordsman."

"I'm not sure, either… I think it's weird, too."

The place was deserted. They didn't see any citizens or even a single Imperial soldier, but the inspection gate was open. As it was, it didn't look like one of the Empire's defensive bases at all.

"Commander Mismis, we need to go farther in…!" In the expanse of the inspection space, Iska gulped when he faintly saw someone farther in the space. "Rin, you keep an eye on Sisbell. Stay here!"

"What? H-hey, Imperial swordsman?!"

He ran into the inspection area.

As the human figures they'd seen steadily grew clearer, he heard Commander Mismis's voice let out a strangled cry from behind him. "How?!"

Dozens of people were collapsed on the ground, both on the Imperial forces' and astral corps' sides. The soldiers were still holding on to their guns, and the astral mages had fallen with their hands outstretched as though they were in the middle of using their powers. There had been no distinction made between who was an Imperial or who was part of the Sovereignty.

They'd all been taken down without discrimination. And among them…

"Looks like there's a familiar face here."

Jhin ran over quickly; then the tip of his shoe tapped a man wearing a mask. It was Lord Mask.

When Jhin saw even one of the Zoa family's purebred types

on the ground, he took on a dubious tone. "If he's here, that must mean all the people on the ground are the Zoa's astral corps. Did they fight the Imperial forces to a draw, then?"

"B-but, Jhin Big Bro, there aren't any signs of a fight!" Nene cautiously approached one of the astral-corps members.

Even when she turned one of them over so their face was upright, she couldn't find a single scratch on them. If they'd fallen from the Imperial forces' shots, then she would have found bullet holes at the very least. In other words...

"They never fought?" Iska murmured, but he still couldn't believe it.

......*We came following Elletear's trail.*

......*If everyone was taken down without discrimination, does that mean she did this?*

She had obliterated the Eight Great Apostles; then she proceeded to destroy the Imperial forces and astral corps. What could her aim be?

"Iska!" Mismis howled.

In the direction the gun-toting commander was looking, a young black-haired girl was walking toward them. Iska recognized her.

"Kissing?!"

"____"

Her face was bare without her usual blindfold. She swayed and made her way over to them.

"Get away from her! Commander, Nene...you too, Jhin!"

"I know," Jhin assured him.

Iska gripped his astral swords, and Jhin aimed his sniper rifle at her. She didn't respond.

Why?

She didn't summon a single thorn like she had at Mudor when

they'd fought last time. Instead, she approached them and continued tottering along.

"Uncle…"

She sank to her knees. The girl crouched over the unconscious Lord Mask as though covering him. It seemed she hadn't even registered that an enemy was in her midst in the first place.

"No…Uncle…wake up! Please…I'm sorry, I'm sorry. I…I was too weak!"

The black-haired girl held the fallen man.

"I was too weak…so you protected me…but you could have escaped! I'm sorry… I'm so sorry, Uncle!"

She continued to cry. Even though she was right in front of Imperial soldiers holding weapons, the girl had forgotten to create her thorns and instead wailed while cradling her guardian.

"Tsk." Jhin lowered his weapon. "Put down your gun, too, Boss. She hasn't even realized we're here. It's better to leave her be than to spur her into action by doing something. We'll catch her later."

"O-okay. Then I'll also—"

"Sister?!"
"Lady Alice?!"

They heard two more shouts at the same time. Those had been Sisbell's and Rin's voices.

Far off from Lord Mask, the two of them ran over somewhere. They ran toward a girl with tousled, long golden hair who had fallen over.

Alice?!

His heart skipped a beat. Why was Alice, who was supposed to be in the Sovereignty, here at the Imperial border? But he put aside that question for later.

CHAPTER 3

"What?!"

As Rin and Sisbell ran off, Iska's eyes automatically followed their backs. He suddenly broke into a cold sweat. The Imperial forces and astral corps were both unconscious for reasons unknown, and even Alice was in the same state. Iska assumed she'd fallen to a similar fate as they had.

......It can't be true.

......Even Alice?!

"Sister! Sister, please!"

"Lady Alice, please wake up! Lady Alice!"

As Sisbell and Rin yelled, they jostled her shoulder.

He didn't know how long they continued, but the golden-haired girl's lips trembled slightly.

"...Uh...ugh."

"Sister?! Rin, did you see her lips move just now?!"

"Yes! Lady Alice, are you all right?!"

"...Uh...cough! ...Cough!"

The golden-haired princess sputtered. After panting roughly for a bit, she slowly opened her eyes.

"...Rin... Sis...bell?"

She hadn't met the same fate as the soldiers around her. Alice had only been temporarily unconscious.

"Lady Alice!" Rin, overcome with emotion, latched on to her mistress. "I was so worried. I'm so glad you're safe... What in the world happened?!"

"It was—"

When Alice tried to explain, her eyes went wide. She'd realized the situation they were in. This was the Empire's checkpoint. And behind Rin and Sisbell was...

......Iska?

* * *

Though she hadn't said it out loud, Iska knew she had just said his name with only her lips.

"We just got here, too…"

He didn't approach her, however. As an Imperial soldier, Iska kept his distance from the princess.

Talking with her, like they had at the Lou family's villa and when they'd recaptured Sisbell, was fine. At the very least, it wouldn't seem odd to the rest of Unit 907.

"What happened here? It's not just the Imperial forces. Dozens of astral-corps members are unconscious. And Lord Mask. You know what happened, don't you?"

"____"

As Rin and Sisbell watched her, Alice silently bit her lip. Sorrow filled her eyes. She looked so weak, Iska doubted his own eyes.

"It was Elletear, wasn't it?"

The voice that had spoken wasn't human.

Alice let out a yelp that wouldn't form into words and flinched when she saw the beastperson appear behind them.

"Oh, how rude of you, Nebulis princess. You do realize the supreme authority of the Empire is before you?"

"You…you're the Lord?!"

"There's no need to be so surprised. I believe you've seen something much worse than me, after all. You witnessed your sister in her monstrous form, didn't you?"

The Lord nonchalantly walked over to them. They seemed to observe Alice as she was sandwiched between Rin and Sisbell.

"Hmm?" Lord Yunmelngen squinted. They had a nostalgic look in their eyes. **"You appear a lot like the first queen, Alicerose. Exactly like her, in fact."**

"……Huh?"

CHAPTER 3

"Regardless. Come, Princess Sisbell, third time's the charm."

"A-again?!" Sisbell hid her chest behind her hand. "I'm exhausted! I've already gone far past the limits of what I'm able to do in a day!"

"I'll take you to an Imperial bakery for cake later."

"No thank you! Oh…it's not that I don't like cake, but if I use Illumination like this, as a repercussion, I won't be able to use my power for several days!"

"But aren't you curious, too?" The Lord swung their arms out; then they looked at the fallen soldiers all around. **"Don't you want to know what happened here? In all likelihood, this was Elletear's rampage, but we need to look into what kind of power that monster has."**

"This really needs to be the last time…" Sisbell placed a hand on her chest and let out a deep breath. "Well, then…"

"Stop!"

They heard a shriek. The black-haired girl had abruptly opened her eyes wide as she still held Lord Mask. Her face was pale, as though all the blood had drained from it, but her shout wasn't directed at Sisbell. What she actually feared was something else.

"It's coming."

A black current formed from thin air.

"A rampage? How uncalled for. I was still very much in control."

The current of air eddied and condensed into a humanoid shape, forming distinct feminine curves until it eventually took the form of a woman with beauty rivaling a goddess.

"…Sis…ter?"

"It's been too long, Sisbell. I'm glad to see you're doing well."

The eldest of the Lou sisters smiled gracefully. She looked at the third sister, who was doing her utmost to simply squeeze out her trembling voice.

"I was so worried when I heard the Hydra family whisked you away. They didn't manhandle you, now, did they?"

"..."

"What's wrong? Why so pale? If you're feeling unwell, just tell me. Oh yes, you must feel so anxious because we're in Imperial land."

"Don't make a fool out of me!" Sisbell bared her teeth and howled. "You're underestimating your own little sister! I know everything... You were the one behind all of it. I know you were behind the Imperial forces attacking the palace. And I know you instructed the Hydra to attack me, too!"

"..."

"You did this here as well, didn't you?!" Her finger quivered slightly as she pointed it at her eldest sibling. "Sister! I don't understand you! Why in the world would you do this...? And you not only made an enemy out of the Empire but of the Sovereignty, too?!"

"Well, they're nothing but nuisances."

"...What?"

"I don't intend to tell you everything. I just explained it to Lord Mask, after all. Oh, I suppose you can't ask him about it anymore, considering the state he's in."

"Sister..." Sisbell was at a loss for words.

Her lips trembled as she backed away. She'd realized the sister in front of her was no longer the sister she knew.

"Nebulis Sovereign First Princess Elletear." The beastperson stepped forward. **"It seems you've been quite consumed already. How does it feel to have become a monster?"**

CHAPTER 3

"Well, it's nice to meet you, Your Excellency." Elletear bowed politely. She even grasped the edge of her skirt and lifted it slightly as though greeting a dance partner. "The Eight Great Apostles have disappeared."

"I know."

"Both the Imperial forces and the astral corps are all sleeping soundly."

"I can see that."

"So…" Elletear traced her own lips with her fingers and lifted a corner of her bewitching mouth. She seemed to be enjoying herself. "After I eliminate everyone here, no one else will be in my way."

"…Huh!" Almost reflexively, Iska unsheathed his astral swords.

Jhin, Commander Mismis, and Nene readied their guns.

I will eliminate you.

They knew it wasn't a joke, especially because they'd seen the battle between the Eight Great Apostles and Elletear using Illumination. She wasn't merely provoking them for nothing. The witch in front of them was simply that dangerous.

"Your Excellency, if I can just make you disappear, my paradise will be all the more reachable."

"Hmm. I don't know about that." Yunmelngen tilted their head. After looking around, they faced Elletear again directly. **"You're late, Crow."**

"Huh?!"

Elletear spun around. There was a black flash that sliced at Elletear's upper body and just barely grazed her.

"How heartless of you. How could you attack a dainty maiden from behind?"

Elletear leaped away. Although she had a large cut on her left shoulder, she didn't bleed a single drop of blood.

"Oh, are you the Black Steel Gladiator Crossweil, by any chance?"

"_____"

The man wore a black coat and held a black unsheathed blade. He didn't respond to Elletear but slowly turned to face the others. "It's exactly how it looks, Iska."

"Master?!"

"This woman isn't human anymore. She can't be called an astral mage, either."

It was black mist. Instead of red blood, black mist seeped from Elletear's wound. In addition to that, the cut itself healed before their eyes. The scene so obviously made it clear that Elletear was no longer human that Alice and Sisbell averted their eyes without realizing it.

"She's completely black inside. Looks like the only thing that's still human about her is her facade."

"Well, that really was uncalled for, sir. But you're not wrong, so I can't deny it." Elletear's smile didn't waver. She seemed to accept being called a monster, almost as though she found it comforting. However… "……Ugh."

Her smile froze. Elletear, who had been watching them calmly, opened her eyes wide and looked up at the deep blue sky.

A tan girl with fluttering dirty-blond hair hovered above them.

The Founder Nebulis.

"Revered Founder?!"

"The Founder?!"

"Oh, it's been a while."

Some yelled in surprise while others yelled in alarm, and one person sighed in resignation, then turned to look at the sky.

CHAPTER 3

On the other hand…

"The astral powers were making a commotion, so I came here to find this…" The girl wasn't looking at anyone in particular. She was watching the black mist spurting from Elletear's shoulder with clear eyes. "So it's you."

She hadn't been looking for a response from the start. She pointed at Elletear.

"Firmament Bloom."

Lightning surged and flashed, swallowing up Elletear entirely and carving a gigantic hole in the asphalt before anyone else could react.

"I intended on destroying the Empire first, but it looks like I'll have to make a change of plans. You are an enemy defiling the planet. Disappear."

"Ah, too bad." The black current swirled. Elletear, who had been obliterated without a trace, reemerged as the black current converged again. "If only I'd been able to get rid of the Lord here, it would have made things so much easier. But the Founder is here with purebred types and the Saint Disciple who inherited the astral swords. I think I've had my fill."

She let out a dramatic sigh.

"So I think I'll make a fresh start."

Elletear's body glowed.

As though she herself were astral power, she suddenly disappeared—or so they all thought. Even Elletear.

Sizzle.

A small spark crackled, and the light around Elletear blew away.

"What?" The first princess's eyes went wide. "Did you interfere with my teleportation…?!"

"You thought I'd let you escape?" The Founder Nebulis's eyes were cold. "I blocked the hole."

"Amazing... So your astral power is related to space-time manipulation. You were a step ahead of me." Elletear smiled bitterly. She didn't have the same composure as before. It was clear she was bluffing and had been cornered.

"You're an eyesore. Disappear, girl."

"Oh, how terrible. What a predicament I've found myself in."

The witch knelt. As though speaking to the depths of the planet, she placed her hands on the ground and caressed it.

—*So please save me—La Selah Milah Uls.*

The ground rumbled as though it were about to overturn itself. A blast of wind began to blow.

"Wh-what is that?! Why is the ground shaking?!"

"Lady Alice, Lady Sisbell, hide! There's something abnormal about this wind!" Rin had invoked her astral power.

The ground at her feet swelled, turning into a golem that shielded Alice and Sisbell. However...the ones who needed protection most of all weren't either of them.

"I see..."

He looked as though he was weak and in pain. When Iska turned around, he saw his teacher on his knees. Behind him...

"Ugh...ah..."

"Your Excellency?!"

Risya was holding the beastperson. Unlike Lord Yunmelngen's normal aloof demeanor, their face had twisted in pain as they held their chest, and their canines peeked from their mouth.

......*What is this? What's going on?*

......*Master?! And the Lord is in pain, too?!*

Iska didn't feel anything strange at all. Neither did Risya, who was holding the Lord. Jhin, Nene, and Commander Mismis, as

CHAPTER 3

well as Alice, Sisbell, and Rin all seemed to wonder why the other two were in pain.

"Now you've done it..." The Founder Nebulis landed on the ground, but it didn't seem intentional. It was as though she'd lost the ability to maintain herself in the air and had fallen. "You woke it? Did you just call the calamity's name?!"

"Ah-ha!" The princess with emerald hair began to laugh. "Ah-ha...ah-ha, ah-ha-ha-ha-ha-ha! What a wonderful day. The two symbols of the Empire and the Sovereignty—the Lord and Revered Founder—are both crawling on the ground!"

It was as though she couldn't stop herself from finding it amusing. She seemed to be caught in a sense of rapture as her face flushed.

"That's right, Revered Founder. The stronger your astral power, the more it rejects the calamity. You likely won't be able to move for a while."

Clack, clack...

As she approached the Founder, her footfalls rang out.

"It's simply not part of my sensibilities to lay a hand on a defenseless person, but you're an exception. I mean, you are a risk factor in my ambitions."

"It's like...you're saying you could get rid of me..."

"Yes, Revered Founder."

As the Founder gritted her teeth, Elletear looked down at her, rapt with attention.

"Once I eliminate you, I'll become the last witch on this planet."

Her body transformed. The body of the princess with the face of a goddess changed before their eyes into a dark, transparent monster.

"You!"

"Are you surprised? Yes, I've already become one with the

calamity to this extent. I could even easily crush you in your weakened form right now, Revered Founder."

Elletear's dark hand reached for her, but before she could touch the defenseless Founder, an ice blade grazed her hand.

"Sister!" The blond girl leaped in front of the immobilized Founder. It was Alice. "Sister, it seems your form is your answer. So you're no longer a Sovereign princess or our kind sister anymore! You are a monster who will wreak havoc on the world! So that is your answer, then!"

Her voice went hoarse from shouting. Her eyes were red and swollen as she pointed at the monster in front of her. "In that case, I will stand against you to protect the Sovereignty!"

An intensely cold breeze began to gust. Vines of ice started to form at a dizzying speed as Alice touched the ground. The broken road froze over, and the vines wrapped around Elletear's legs. "Lock!"

"My, my, Alice."

Crack.

The ice began to crack. It was the sound not of Elletear freezing but of the ice around her legs shattering.

"How?!"

"What a quaint girl you are. So you're still holding back on me."

Then she disappeared. She left not a sound or a trace.

"She's gone?"

"Oh, a split end."

"Eek?!" Alice's face froze. Her sister had reappeared right next to her and was caressing her hair.

"It's very damaged. This is no good, Alice. You must take care of your hair."

"Ugh!"

CHAPTER 3

"But I'll make sure you don't have to worry about it ever again."

The witch's fingertips were black and transparent. They crawled up Alice's neck like five small serpents.

"I'm sorry, Alice. This is where you'll..."

"I'd never allow you to do that!"

Elletear's fingers were still intertwined around Alice's neck, but before she could strangle Alice, Iska swung his sword, though he swiped only at the spot Elletear had been.

She had instantly teleported.

Elletear disappeared before Iska could even touch her with his sword.

......*It's the same as before. There's almost no sign of when she's going to teleport.*

......*It's the same as Kelvina's phototeleportation leaps!*

She was almost astral power itself. The laws of physics didn't apply to Elletear as she was now.

"Alice!" He ran toward Elletear, who had appeared in front of him.

Iska yelled at Alice behind him, "Use your ice to capture her again."

"What? B-but...!"

"There's a weakness to Elletear's teleportation. She can't use it when she's restrained by astral energy."

That had been the case with Kelvina. Because she'd been held down by Rin's golem, she hadn't been able to make a leap and had fallen to the ground. A moment would be enough. He just needed her to hold Elletear down with her ice vines.

"I won't let her escape this time."

"**Oh, are you confessing your love for me now?**"

She was calm and composed, but Elletear teleported again farther back.

CHAPTER 3

She was obviously different. She didn't hide her heavy caution that she hadn't shown when facing the Lord, the Founder, or Alice.

"Ah, that hurt…"

A small bit of her side was missing from her transparent black body.

It was where she'd been cut by the astral sword. She still hadn't been able to recover from the wound.

"It's just like Kelvina said. My natural enemy would be incredibly pure astral energy. And if the astral swords are the most potent form of it, I see that it's true. It seems even touching it is dangerous for me."

"I'm sure I told you before…"

He leaped from the ground. Iska ran closer to her quickly enough that Elletear couldn't read how far apart they were for a moment.

"How quick you are…"

"There won't be a next time."

He would stop her before she could use her powers. In other words, he would win by being the first to strike. That was a tactic that worked with any astral mage, no matter how powerful, including Elletear. But nevertheless…

"I wanted to be in exactly this situation." The monster's voice grew louder. **"Even in this form, even if I'm hated by so many, I have a knight who will protect me. Oh, how wonderful it feels to be a princess with a knight in shining armor who comes running to her rescue… I'm truly so happy…"**

This is why I love you, Joheim.

Iska raised his astral sword.

Before it could touch Elletear, though, a sword from the side thrust out to stop him.

"What?!"

"She is my master, so keep your hands off her, please."

It was a red-haired Imperial soldier. Iska thought the man's battle uniform, which seemed to be a cross between a coat and armor, was incredibly familiar. That was because he had been one of Iska's colleagues.

The Saint Disciple of the first seat, the "Flash" Knight Joheim. This man had always been Elletear's and had joined the Imperial forces with the intention of betraying the Empire. Sisbell's Illumination power had revealed it.

But when Iska thought about it, he'd had a clue right from the start that this was the case. He had gotten it from Elletear.

"There was a time when I was close with the Imperial army."

"I would love to know. There are two people who wield swords among the eleven Saint Disciples. I wonder who would be stronger: you or Joheim?"

Elletear had been secretly communicating with someone in the Imperial forces. And she had blatantly disclosed that it was Joheim.

…Wait.

……Does that mean she already saw through things up to this point back then?!

There were only two Saint Disciples who were swordsmen. In other words, Elletear had predicted the two of them would fight someday to see who was stronger.

And Iska had replied to her in the past…

* * *

"I specialize in anti-astral mage techniques. I never trained to fight against people."

"Even if I competed, I would fall behind at the first or second strike, and I'd lose at the third."

"Oh, Joheim, I was wondering where you had gone." With the help of Risya's hand. the Lord stood back up. **"I knew you weren't being honest. I thought you were a spy for the Sovereignty, but I see you were on that *thing's* side."**

"I would thank you for all you've done for me, Your Excellency…but alas," the First Saint Disciple answered with a serious expression. "I approached you in order to obtain information. And you made me a Saint Disciple in order to obtain information from me. We owe nothing to each other. And please do not call my master *that thing*."

"Look for yourself, Joheim. That thing standing behind you is even more of a monster than I am."

"There is no monster here." The knight moved to stand in front of the dark witch to protect her. "I only see a princess with ideals nobler than anyone else's."

"Were you brainwashed?"

"Of course not." The one to answer was the monster behind him. **"I rejected Joheim multiple times. I told him I was a monster, that the world would hate me, but he never left me. That's all."**

Then she went silent. Joheim simply raised his sword as Elletear remained behind him. Both of them were staring at the other side and didn't move.

……*Elletear is after the Lord and Founder.*

……*But I'm standing in front with the astral swords. And Alice is behind me.*

CHAPTER 3

They were at a stalemate. Elletear couldn't attack recklessly. On the other hand, if Iska tried to attack, the Saint Disciple was in his way.

They were at an impasse.

In order to break through it, he needed an overbearing offense or...

"Hmm... Looks like this is over."

Clap.

Elletear had signaled for her guard to retreat.

"Let's withdraw, Joheim. I'll see the rest of you sooner or later."

She turned away. It was almost as though the tension had never existed in the first place.

"I'll gain much more power from the planet's core; then, once I've evolved, we'll meet again."

"Huh? Are you running away, Sister?!"

"Yes, I am, Alice. Unlike you, I'm used to running rather than fighting. Oh, but I have thought of something I could tease you with."

Elletear turned around. From her outstretched fingers, two dark droplets of water fell and splashed as they hit the ground.

"Alice, have you ever fought astral power before?"

"What?"

"Eidos of the sea and eidos of the earth. You can't let them escape. Just one of these could destroy the whole Empire and Sovereignty."

Splish.

Elletear and Joheim seemed to sink into the shadows at their feet and disappeared.

Then, as though to replace them, the black droplets of water rose, forming into two monsters.

......*Those.*
......*What are those?!*

It sent shudders down Iska's spine, and he broke out into goose bumps. He felt a sense of emptiness greater than he'd ever felt before against any other enemy he'd faced.

The monsters, glowing ominously, took on the shape of humans.

"_____"
"_____"

One was a dark blue that no light could penetrate, like the depths of the ocean. The other was dark red like corrupted soil. In their hands, they held cross-shaped spears that looked as though they could have been made of solid seawater and solid blood. Their heads were perfectly round without any indents at all. Only the spot where their eyes should've been was devoid of light, so he couldn't even see where they were looking.

The monsters creaked like an old door as their faces slowly turned toward Iska. He felt an unbelievable sense of hostility coming from them.

"Um, Iska…"

"Stay back, Sisbell!" He readied his astral swords in his hands and yelled, "They're no normal opponents!"

"Lady Elletear, what kind of joke is this…?" Rin muttered.

In order to keep his distance from the two monsters, Iska slowly backed away.

"These could destroy the Sovereignty on their own? How could she even joke about that?!"

"You don't need to think about what she said, Rin." Next to her, Alice firmly bit her lip. "She's now an enemy of the Sovereignty.

CHAPTER 3

Just take it as simple provocation. We need to get rid of these monsters quickly. At least, I hope we will…"

She didn't let the monsters out of her sight.

"So let's say you truly are the Lord. I don't intend to harm the Empire here today. So—?" Alice quickly asked the beastperson.

"Keep your eyes ahead. This is a battlefield," the Lord said without leniency as the blue giant—the eidos of the sea—attacked Alice.

It glided across the ground, seeming to travel sluggishly, though it slipped along like a skater on ice and approached her at an alarming speed.

"Blade!" The water waiting at hand solidified before their eyes. The sword Alice had formed using her astral power thrust through the giant's breast as it charged toward her. Or so it seemed.

That was how it looked to Iska as he watched the entire thing happen from start to finish.

The ice sword that Alice had thrown pierced through the eidos of the sea. But now it flew toward Alice.

"What?"

Her astral power's automatic defenses didn't activate. Because Alice had created the sword, her astral powers didn't sense it as a threat.

Zoosh…

The ice blade made a dull sound as it pierced something. Just before it could harm Alice, a golem had appeared to protect her, and the blade was now deeply embedded in it.

"Lady Alice, get back!"

"Guh?!" Alice leaped without worrying about grace. Her expression quickly turned grim. "It deflected my astral power's attack?!"

With that single exchange, she understood what happened.

The monster could interfere with astral power. It seemed that was what the eidos could do. It likely could reflect astral powers in the same way a mirror could reflect light.

That was an astral mage's worst enemy. However...

Even when faced with such a formidable foe, Rin had been quick on her feet.

"Knock it back!" Rin ordered.

The golem raised its arms and hit the giant heading toward Alice.

Crack.

When the golem's fist made contact with the eidos, a small fissure formed in it.

"I knew it! It can only repel astral energy!"

Ice astral mages created ice, but earth astral mages manipulated soil. Since Rin was manipulating real dirt, and the golem was made up of it, the eidos couldn't repel its attacks. It seemed physical destruction would work. So to defeat the eidos, they simply needed to use something other than pure astral power.

"Guns! This is our time to shine, Imperial soldiers!"

"Is it, though?" Only Iska, who was the closest to him, had overheard Jhin's muttering. "Boss, Nene, stop."

"Huh?!"

"Why, Jhin?!" Nene said.

"I'll shoot it." Jhin didn't wait for them to respond and had his gun at the ready. He had taken aim at the other monster. The red giant was quickly sliding across the ground toward Unit 907. He fired at its knee.

Blood splattered. The bullet that they were sure had hit the eidos had instead shot through Jhin's shoulder.

"Jhin?!"

"Don't shoot, Boss! Just like I thought, this is bad. I don't know how it works, though!" Jhin held his wound and withdrew. Blood dripped onto the ground as he walked. "The red one reflects physical attacks."

The eidos of the sea reflected astral energy.
The eidos of the earth reflected physical impulses.

As one giant reflected astral energy, they could figure out what the other one did. So any bullets would be sent flying back. They couldn't even use Imperial artillery on it.
 …… *That's why Jhin was quick to act.*
 …… *He made sure to calculate everything out with that one shot.*
That was why he'd aimed for the knee.
Jhin had anticipated the bullet might ricochet, so he'd calculated the angle and made sure it would only graze his shoulder.
"These monsters really have inconvenient abilities…!" Rin gritted her back teeth.
These were their natural enemies. Astral mages were made powerless when faced with the eidos of the sea. The Imperial forces were powerless when faced with the eidos of the earth. Elletear hadn't been lying at all. Each of them had the potential to single-handedly destroy the Empire and the Sovereignty.
"But all we have to do is trade targets!" Commander Mismis changed her aim as she held her handgun. She pointed it at the eidos of the sea. The gun would work on the blue giant.
"We'll take this one!"
But before she could shoot, the two giants began to chant, almost as though they were reciting a witch's spells.
—"**Corna killsies. Flame/Blue.**"
—"**Ryphe fulis. Lightning/Red.**"
Light and flames issued forth. From a fissure in the ground,

ferocious blue sparks started to burst from blue flames. From a tear in the clouds, there came an intense rumble of thunder and a red lightning bolt. Both rushed at them with the force of an avalanche. The atmosphere was scorched, and the road burned as they swallowed everything up.

There was no way to run from it. The scope was vast and would soon swallow the entire area. The moment they realized that, Iska and Alice moved at the same time.

"Wall!"

"Get back!"

The wall of ice Alice created stopped the flames. Iska used a dent in the wall as a foothold to leap into the air.

As the lightning fell, faster than the human eye could perceive, his instincts told him where it would strike, and he raised his astral sword. "Hyah!"

He managed to catch the edge of the lightning bolt with his sword. When the sword met the red flash of light, it broke into several more bolts and disappeared as though melting into the air. However...

He hadn't managed to sever it. The sword had only split part of it. Being able to slice through lightning was an act far beyond normal human ability, so Iska had mostly relied on instinct.

The lightning he'd failed to cut had broken into more bolts, one of which raced toward the girl with strawberry-blond hair behind him.

"No, Sisbell!"

"Huh?!"

Sisbell didn't even have time to scream. She only opened her eyes wide in fear as lightning pursued her like it was going after its prey.

"Foolish pupil." A flash struck down the lightning. Crossweil had stepped in front of Sisbell and stopped it. "You're forcing me out of retirement."

"Uh, um…thank you…?"

"Yunmelngen." As Crossweil gripped his sword, which looked similar to the astral swords, he bluntly called the Lord. "Get rid of some people."

"You're so benevolent, Crow." The beastperson smiled weakly, still in Risya's arms. **"I'm counting on you, astral powers. Please move everyone I count seven hundred meters away from here. Crow, Princess Sisbell, and me."**

"Wh-what?! Wh-what are you doing?!"

"And…" The Lord ignored Sisbell and turned around. They pointed at the many people who had collapsed on the ground. **"Also all those humans."**

Fwoom.

A viscous white wall of liquid groaned as it spread around. The sight was unusual to see, but if the Lord's words were to be taken as true, the wall was actually a group of astral powers that made up the Planet's Defense.

"This is a special service for you, Princess Aliceliese. I'll transport your soldiers as well. And your sister. They'd be a burden, after all."

"Huh?! Wh-who's a burden?! I am—"

"Move us."

The Lord snapped their fingers.

The white substance turned into a curtain of light. It engulfed the Lord, Crossweil, Sisbell, and all the other people and teleported them out of the checkpoint.

"Wait, Your Excellency, are you leaving me to work overtime?!" Risya smiled wanly. "How inconsiderate. I'm supposed to be your staff officer. I'm not meant to be on the front lines. I should be in a nice, air-conditioned office, sipping coffee—"

"Shut up and move," Rin shouted. She raised her skirt and gripped a dagger that had been hidden under it in her hand. "Lady Alice, the woman in glasses is able to use artificial astral power. Think of it as an ability that can bind its target. It's specialized to provide support."

"Did you just reveal the secret behind my astral power?!"

"You and Lady Alice can take the red one. I'll handle this one."

The flames were raging. The blue fire scattered around, trying to engulf the inspection area. It leaped from the paved road to the grass. Dense smoke began to rise from all over.

The battlefield had been divided in two.

The eidos of the sea against Rin and Iska's unit.
The eidos of the earth against Alice and Risya.

"Rin!" Alice yelled as blue sparks flitted about. "Don't worry about me! You need to take care of your—"

"**Veiz—claw.**"

"Huh?!"

A cross-shaped spear flew through the air. While Alice had been distracted by her concerns about Rin, the red giant had thrown a spear at her.

"Entangle!" Ice vines rose from the ground and grabbed the spear in midair. She watched the spear break apart into dirt and fall back to the soil from the corner of her eye. "It's rude to interrupt a lady. If you're truly my sister's subordinates, you would do well to—"

"**Veiz—claw.**"

"……Guh! You really are rude!"

CHAPTER 3

The eidos summoned another spear. With that in its hand, it charged at Alice with terrifying vigor.

...... So that's what this is. They don't have any intelligence.

...... They're just beasts after blood!

Since they were Elletear's creations, she'd assumed they'd be intelligent, but they were barbarians. Their only reason for existence seemed to be to destroy anything on the planet when they appeared.

"Then I won't show you any mercy, either!"

Ice Calamity—Blizzard of a Thousand Thorns!

Several hundred ice swords appeared and covered the sky. Even more appeared on the ground. They even formed on an already frozen bench, fully enveloping the giant.

"Pierce it!" The ice swords rained down like a downpour.

In that moment, the red giant went into motion. It raised the spear in its hand and swiped at the air, creating a whirlwind.

Fwoosh!

The air seemed to shriek. The ice swords headed for the eidos were caught in the tempest and blown away like leaves in the wind.

"No way...?!"

It hadn't used any special ability, technique, or move. It was just swinging its spear and using brute strength to blast away the swords.

It had supernatural strength. She had no idea how much strength it would take to create such a natural disaster through sheer force.

When Alice realized the spear was aimed at her breast, all the blood seemed to drain from her body. This was bad.

"Vines, stop it!"

The eidos charged with its spear in hand. It slid across the ground with enough force to send the pavement flying in its wake.

In an attempt to stop the giant, Alice ordered the ice vines to entangle themselves around it.

Or that was what she'd intended.

Crack...

Right in front of Alice's eyes, the ice vines were torn to shreds.

The giant didn't stop its charge. It easily broke through the ice wall and brought the red spear down toward Alice—but it missed.

The eidos of the earth stopped.

It'd just been about to bring down its spear. Though it was almost invisible, the red giant's knees and neck were entangled in several threads thinner than strands of hair.

The astral threads, which were far thinner than the ice vines, tangled around the eidos and didn't let go.

"Well... If it's the Lord's order, I suppose I must comply."

From a distance away from Alice, Risya, who seemed to have been watching from afar, spread her arms slowly. A small glowing orb unraveled in the air into threads and traveled along the ground. "This is Spun, my fourth-generation astral power. Well, we're supposed to hate each other, but shall we cooperate just this once, Miss Ice Calamity Witch?"

"..."

"Oh, do you not like being called a witch? It just slipped out."

"...No."

Risya wore an incredibly sarcastic smile. Alice gave her a genuine smile in response. "Thank you. You saved me."

"Well, if you'd make it quick, then. While I still have the giant caught. Shrink!"

Creak.

The threads around the eidos's neck dug in. Though the threads

CHAPTER 3

were thin, they were mighty enough to hold back the supernaturally strong and violent giant.

Right at that moment...the ice sword that Alice threw pierced the eidos.

"Urgh!"

It howled in rage. This time, the attack had worked. It seemed that Alice's astral power, which the eidos of the sea had reflected, was the eidos of the earth's weak point.

"Keep it there! Hold it there!"

"Of course. It's difficult to lay down the work to use Spun, but once someone is caught, it's like you've as good as won. So please go ahead and... Hmm?"

Something was off.

She felt a very minute amount of resistance from the threads wrapped around the red giant, but something was strange about how it felt in a way she couldn't describe. Risya narrowed her eyes.

It felt as though the threads were slipping.

The resistance from the threads was progressively getting weaker, as though she had caught water or air. She was sure she had the eidos of the earth restrained.

"I don't have a great feeling about this. Princess Aliceliese, if you're going to finish it off, you should do it quickly—"

Something changed.

As Risya was speaking, the red giant started to transform.

Eighth checkpoint, north side.

The blue sparks were still sputtering in the area and scorching the lawn.

"Another one!" Rin touched the ground with her hand. The

soil writhed and turned into a second golem. "It's just as you can see. After getting hit with the golem, the monster's exterior started to crack. It can't be defeated with astral power, but it doesn't like physical attacks!"

"And it doesn't look like it's regenerating, either!" Nene added. She leveled her gun at the blue giant—the eidos of the sea. "If we just keep firing at it, we should be able to easily destroy it. Commander!"

"R-right!" Nene and Commander Mismis stood beside each other. Jhin readied his sniper rifle behind them, and Iska took the forefront to complete their formation.

"Imperial swordsman."

"Okay."

Rin and the golem ran at the blue giant, taking the most direct path, followed by Iska.

......*Rin's daggers and the golem's fists.*

......*And my astral swords. All of these are basically poison to the giant.*

They'd be fatal blows. He was sure the eidos couldn't allow them to hit it if it wanted to survive.

So what would it do? Would it try to counterattack or dodge them?

......*If it tries to intercept us with the blue flames, then I'll cut through those using my astral sword.*

......*If it tries to dodge us, the commander, Nene, and Jhin will shoot it.*

They had an overwhelming advantage in this game. Regardless of what it did, it was cornered. Iska and everyone else had imagined that would be happening soon...

"Corna killsies. Flame/Blue."

"The flames! Rin, stop!"

CHAPTER 3

He took Rin's place at the forefront. As the roaring blue flames whirled in front of him, Iska took another step forward. He swiped at the flames using his astral sword. However...its target was neither Iska nor Rin, or even Unit 907 behind them.

The giant itself was on fire.

In an instant, the blue giant was fully engulfed in flames.
"What?!"
He reflexively stopped. Of course, he couldn't approach the fire recklessly, but there were also alarm bells ringing, telling him not to move closer. And in that moment, the flames surged, charring the road, swallowing the bench, spreading more and more.
"Is it self-destructing?"
"No..."
He felt cold sweat form on his face. The blue giant was engulfed in the raging inferno and disappeared from view.
"It's camouflage!"
"What?"
"Rin, protect yourself with the golem!"
The fire roared.
The flames burst next to Rin.
The fire undulated wildly, and the blue giant leaped out from the flames.
"What?! Golem!" Rin sent the golem off, and she leaped into the air. The giant swung its shining spear and broke the golem into pieces.
"It's maneuvering in the flames!"
Right after Jhin, Commander Mismis and Nene fired their weapons, the three bullets all cutting through the air, but by the time they had been fired, the giant had already disappeared back into the fire.

......The giant covered itself in blue flames so it can hide itself and approach us.

......This goes beyond camouflage. It assimilated with the flames!

"Guh!"

The raging fire didn't stop spreading even when he sliced at the flare closest to him.

From the grass to the trees one after another, the flames rapidly spread, and the area that the eidos could freely move around in was increasing.

......Maybe Alice could do it?

......Maybe Alice's ice could extinguish the flames?!

No, it was no use. The eidos of the sea reflected astral energy. If she unleashed the frost needed to extinguish all the flames and it was reflected, they would be the ones suffering casualties.

"Jhin Big Bro! Can you shoot into the flames?!"

"I can't follow it. There's too much blocking my line of sight."

He meant the roaring flames and the heat wave coming off them. He couldn't keep track of where the eidos had traveled within the flames. Even the sparks in the air were obstructing his vision.

"Nene, don't go near the flames. You won't know when the monster will leap out of them!"

"I—I know that, but...but the fire is spreading...!" Nene backed away. Even as she did that, the flames slowly crept toward her. It was trying to surround them in all directions.

"Tsk. Get back, Boss!"

"_____"

"Hey, Boss? ...Boss?"

Jhin turned to look to the side.

Commander Mismis was standing stock-still. She was murmuring something to herself as though she was in a trance and

CHAPTER 3

hadn't noticed the flames coming at her. "…Flames? …Surrounded? …Huh…uh…uh…"

"Hey, Boss, what's wrong?!"

"Right… What did I do…in Alsamira…?"

She didn't respond even when Jhin grabbed her shoulder. She seemed to have forgotten to even blink as she turned toward the raging flames.

"Boss, get back!"

"You're in danger, Commander!"

Jhin grabbed her right hand and Nene her left hand, and they pulled. Commander Mismis fell backward. With hardly a moment to spare, the eidos's spear lunged from the flames where she had been. If the other two hadn't acted, Mismis would have been skewered without putting up any resistance, but she still seemed to be in a daze.

"Imperial swordsman! What happened to your commander?!" Rin shouted.

"I'm not sure, either. Commander Mismis, what happened?!"

"……Ugh." Commander Mismis's eyes opened wide in surprise. It wasn't because Iska had called her, however. She was still staring into the flames.

"So E lu emne xel noi Es—accept me?"

"Commander?!"

"No, wait, Imperial swordsman. I can't believe it's happening right at this moment…"

Rin held her breath. She watched as Mismis grasped her left shoulder—her astral crest.

"It's started to awaken!"

She was awakening as an astral mage? As an Imperial, Iska had no idea whether this was good or bad, considering the situation. Rin, meanwhile, was scowling.

"This is terrible timing. When an astral mage awakens, they hear a voice from their astral power. And during that moment, they lose consciousness, like they're in a dream. She's defenseless!"

"What?!"

Now that she had told him this, he remembered something similar he'd seen in the past from a century ago that Sisbell's Illumination power had re-created. The Founder Eve's awakening had been similar.

"Who am I?"

"......Huh? Come on, what are you saying? Eve?!"

"Wh...what am I...h-human...or astral power...?"

She hadn't even woken up when her brother had called her.

He saw the Founder in Commander Mismis at that moment.

......The timing is horrible, just like Rin said.

......Why is this happening while we're fighting?!

The flames howled, relentlessly bellowing as the sparks flew all around and the heat wave pushed at them, threatening to burn them.

It also headed straight for the defenseless Commander Mismis.

"Commander Mismis!"

"Commander, move!"

Rin reached out, and Iska held the astral swords as he stood to block it.

A wave of blue flames approached them.

And...

...then it disappeared.

"......Huh?"

Iska kept a tight hold of his sword as he blinked.

CHAPTER 3

What in the world had happened?

The flames surrounding them shrank before their eyes. Even the heat that blistered their skin subsided. The wind was no longer scorching hot. The heat wave that had once made them break out into a sweat had turned into a gentle spring breeze.

"Is it the boss…?!" Jhin's throat was hoarse as he yelled. "The same thing happened in Alsamira! Iska, this breeze is the boss's astral power!"

"It is?!"

Above their heads, a bluish-green twinkling light flickered and whirled around, filling the air. It was the same color as the astral crest on Mismis's shoulder.

"Wind astral power? What kind of technique is this? Why are the eidos's flames disappearing?!" Rin yelled as she looked up at the sky.

Iska had the same questions. Even after his master's extensive education about astral powers, he couldn't think of any that fit this description. However…

"We'll figure it out later…!"

As the flames burst, Iska spun like a top. He headed for the eidos of the sea. The heat and sparks disappeared. The flames shrank, and their surface area dwindled, so he could sense where his opponent was.

"Jhin!"

"There!" Jhin fired. The bullet pierced through the blue flames and headed deep within to pierce the monster hiding inside.

"——!" It howled in rage.

The flames wavered. The giant appeared from the flames like a fog had cleared.

"Corna killsies. Flame/Blue."

"It's trying it again? Don't let it escape!"

Rin threw both daggers in her hands. The golem made from earth jumped off the ground, creating a tremor as it did and flinging its fist at the eidos of the sea. Just one more...

With one more strike, its cracked body would shatter into shards like glass. The moment that strike connected...

Something changed—in that second, the blue giant transformed right before their very eyes.

It turned red.

It shifted from a transparent, sealike blue into a muddy, earthy red. It was so sudden that it seemed like it had occurred in a single instant.

"Impossible!"

Rin's face froze.

The eidos had turned red.

The moment the golem's fist made contact, its arm exploded from the elbow down, turning into clumps of dirt. The impact had been repelled. Without a doubt, it had turned into an eidos of the earth that deterred all physical attacks.

"Rin, stop!"

"Guh...!" Rin crossed her arms and instantly created a shield of soil to cover her face. A dagger embedded into it as well. The eidos had sent it flying back, of course.

"How?!" Nene lowered her gun in a panic.

Their bullets wouldn't work on a red giant. If they shot at it, the bullet would only ricochet and come back to injure them.

"There are two red giants now?!"

"No, look more closely, Nene."

Jhin used his muzzle to point at the eidos's legs and shoulders.

CHAPTER 3

Ice swords were piercing it. The threads from Risya's astral power were wrapped around its neck.

"It traded places with the one back there!"

The two eidoses were two and also one. They could sense when the other was in trouble and switch places. In other words, the one that Alice and Risya were fighting now…

There was a scream.

It had come from deeper in the grounds.

He thought he heard Alice scream in pain from far off, where he shouldn't have been able to hear her.

No astral power existed that could reflect other powers. And no weapons existed that could, either.

And as for Alice, she'd never experienced something exactly like her own astral power charging back at her on the battlefield.

"How?!"

It had turned from red to blue. Dozens of ice blades were flying down when the eidos of the earth had turned into the color of the eidos of the sea right in front of Alice's eyes.

The moment those touched the eidos of the sea, they were all sent flying back in various directions.

"Ugh, shield!"

The towering ice that formed stopped the blades flying at her. Ice clashed with ice. White frost swept over them, and everything around was cloaked in white mist like a night of the midnight sun.

"Well, you saved me, Princess. I almost ended up skewered by the ice, too."

"I suppose…I should reconsider using astral attacks that are too powerful…"

The ice tower was filled with holes.

She glared at the eidos through one gap and felt her left elbow with her hand. She found a slightly red and swollen cut there. There had been too many ice blades flying back that the ice wall she had made so suddenly hadn't been able to fully protect her.

……*I can't believe I've been hurt by my own powers.*

……*I feel so ashamed; it's a wound to my psyche, too.*

"What about your threads?"

"They're no longer useful."

Risya tried to manipulate them, but the threads, which had become stretched like overused rubber bands, slipped back into her palms. "I was wondering how my threads would be repelled. But it looks like they were the moment they touched the thing."

Astral powers wouldn't work on the eidos of the sea. Alice's ice and Risya's threads were no exception.

"I've figured out something. That giant doesn't have a specific weakness. No matter where we attack it, it repels them."

"So you've given up?"

"I don't think so—wall, spring forth!"

She raised her right hand. At Alice's command, an ice wall as large as a skyscraper rose. It had become an ice prison for the eidos.

"But it can't reflect anything if we don't hit it. We can simply trap it."

"Oh? And then what?"

"Run!"

Follow me, Alice seemed to signal with her eyes as she ran through the frozen grounds. "While it's trapped, we'll trade places. We'll take the red, and Iska's group will take the blue. The one that we're best suited for."

CHAPTER 3

"But if we switch places, won't the enemy, too?"

"It can't. It can't do it again. It either has some sort of condition it needs to fulfill in order to or it has to wait a certain amount of time before it can do it again."

The same applied to Alice's Great Ice Calamity. Her powerful technique, which had inspired her other title, had one hidden condition, which was that her surroundings needed to already be cooled to a certain temperature. She also couldn't use it several times in a row. It required a one-hour cooldown at minimum before she could use it again. Astral power wasn't inexhaustible.

"If it could do it again, it would have switched places the moment Rin's golem first hit it. But it didn't. It kept it as a last resort."

"I see. How astute of you." As Risya kept pace with her, she looked at Alice with admiration. "I'll refrain from saying that a witch princess like you should know, considering you're a monster like it."

"You call that refraining?"

"Yes. Also, you specified we would take the red one and that Iska's group would handle the blue giant. Why specify Iska rather than Rin?"

"Urgh?!" She let out a sound that didn't form into words. She hadn't even noticed it herself. She knew better than anyone how powerful Iska was, so she ended up saying his name.

"Are you acquainted with him?"

"There's nothing between us! Uh, earlier I, uh… Ugh, this is such trouble. This isn't the time for—"

"Corna killsies. Flame/Blue."

There was a blast. Behind Alice and Risya, flames had broken the ice cage and sent splinters flying.

"It already broke out of it?!"

The eidos of the sea leaped from the cage.
The giant disappeared into the raging flames.

Then it leaped out from the flames right next to Alice.

"Huh?! It overtook us?!"

It had teleported within the flames. The spreading blue fire was the eidos of the sea's territory. It seemed the giant could travel within the flames.

"So it won't let us go, then… That's how much it doesn't want us to switch places."

The blue giant stood in their way. As Alice looked up at the giant bathed in fierce flames, she sighed. "I see. In that case—"

A shot rang out.

She heard it from far, far off.

Eighth checkpoint, north side.

A strange hex unlike anything they'd heard before rang out.

"Ryphe fulis, Lightning/Red."

From a rift in the clouds, red lightning rained down and tore through the air.

"That lightning! Imperial swordsman!"

"Get down!"

At Rin's order, the earth heaved. Iska leaped off the slope and flew through the air. As he fell in a straight line, his blade flashed, and he focused himself entirely on bringing his sword down.

The blade swiped through the lightning.

"Veiz—claw."

CHAPTER 3

"Huh?!"

It was the red spear.

Things had gone according to plan until Iska had cut through the lightning. The eidos had timed right then to throw its spear at him. Just before it hurled at him, a bullet shot through the spear's point.

"Iska Big Bro!"

"You saved me, Nene!"

When he landed on the ground, he leaped again. He charged toward the giant as it made a new spear.

"_____"

As soon as it noticed Iska approaching, it stopped forming the spear and backed away immediately.

"So it's the astral swords, then."

He knew it.

It had basically been intuition to Iska, but it seemed that even though the eidos repelled physical attacks, the swords would work on it. When Iska approached it, the eidos had reacted as though it dreaded him, which was proof enough.

......*If the astral swords have an effect on it...*

......*then this is no different from fighting an astral mage!*

He headed toward his enemy again. He would clear away all it threw at him and wouldn't let it attack in order to make this a quick and decisive battle. However...

One unforeseen circumstance had made his tactic crumble.

"...Uh...ah...!"

He heard a voice that was on the verge of disappearing. Iska, Jhin, Nene, and Rin all watched as the small commander fell to her knees.

"Commander?!"

Rin, who was closest, reached out, then hesitated. They were right in front of the eidos's eyes. If she grabbed Commander Mismis, Rin would be defenseless. Rin had to choose between grabbing her or abandoning her. Rin's hesitation likely hadn't lasted more than a fraction of a second.

"Ugh, damn it!" Rin grabbed Commander Mismis and fell.

As the eidos looked down at Rin, who had her hands full and was defenseless, it brought down its spear, aiming for Rin's head.

"You know what to do!"

"I know!"

There was a clear sound.

Iska stopped the tip of the spear using his astral sword. The sword and spear collided and gnashed like nails scraping against glass.

"Rin, get back with the commander!"

"No, stay right there." As Iska and the eidos were locked together, a voice came from right beside them. "No one move. Iska, you keep that thing in check."

"Jhin?!"

"The boss did her job. Now it's our turn." Jhin got his sniper ready. He aimed the muzzle straight for the eidos. Everyone doubted their eyes. Bullets would be sent flying back…

"Jhin Big Bro?!"

"Stop! What are you thinking?!"

"―――"

Nene and Rin yelled at him, but the silver-haired sniper said nothing in response. Rather, he hadn't even heard them. Even Iska opened his eyes wide as he watched, and the sniper continued to stare at the red giant with utmost concentration.

"Imperial weapons won't work on this monster. It repels everything."

"Jhin Big Bro?! Th-that's right! So―"

"So why not?"

CHAPTER 3

A gunshot rang out. As he spoke, the bullet traveled through the air. It collided with the eidos, then ricocheted. The bullet grazed Jhin's cheek, then went between Nene and Rin and continued deeper into the space.

It pierced the eidos of the sea.

What in the world had happened?
All of them doubted their eyes. The eidos of the earth that had been shot doubtlessly was still trying to understand it, too. The eidos of the sea that had been pierced by the returning bullet probably had no idea what hit it.

"Basically..." The sniper, who had single-handedly used the eidos of the earth to make his shot, nodded matter-of-factly. "I just checked the angle of reflection."

"——!" They heard the eidos's death throes.

Crick...crack...

Fragments of light broke off from the shot eidos and fell one after another.

However...the monster had yet to fall. Though its body was crumbling apart, it leaped into the fire and disappeared. Right after that, the flames still raging behind Rin and the unconscious Commander Mismis wavered.

"Rin, behind you!"

The eidos of the sea attacked. The spearhead split in two. Each half headed toward Rin and Commander Mismis.

"That's my colleague!"

"That's my attendant!"

The spear cut through thin air. Threads had grabbed the two immobile women and pulled them back. The spear was also stopped by a wall of ice that jutted out from the ground.

CHAPTER 3

"Looks like you had an easy job, Ms. Saint Disciple."

"And looks like you did a great job, Jhin-Jhin."

Risya continued to manipulate the threads. Alice walked over from behind her, her hair fluttering in the wind.

"Tsk!"

The eidos of the sea collapsed. Its body went up in flames. Its blue body turned into blue flames—it was self-destructing. As its body was used as the fuel for the fierce fire, it fell over, trying to bring Rin and Commander Mismis down with it. But...

"Iska!"

"Right."

He didn't need to be told. Alice's voice pressed him on as he swung his black astral blade and cut down the burning eidos in one stroke.

"____"

The eidos of the sea vanished.

But the battle wasn't over yet.

There was another one. The eidos of the earth was still mostly unharmed.

"Come, divine staff."

High in the sky, a youthful voice of depths unknown incanted a spell, and everyone turned to her automatically.

Yes.

The strongest and greatest astral mage was with them now that they all thought about it.

"How troublesome. Is this not over yet?"

It was the Founder Nebulis.

The small girl raised her right hand and created a twisted black staff.

It couldn't be...

"Wait, Nebulis?!"

"This will be my single act of kindness. Get down."

Get down!

They had no time to check who had said it as all of them dove to the ground. They got as low as they could and as far as they could from the eidos, covering their ears and closing their eyes.

The divine staff fell from the sky.

The atmosphere seemed to shriek. With a rumble like the world was ending, the ground broke apart, and both wind and a shock wave of equal parts extreme heat and intense cold violently swept over the area as the staff fell.

There was a gigantic flash of light and a shock wave.

And though they closed their eyes, they almost fell unconscious from the impact.

"..."

Iska opened his eyes. A gigantic crater had been left behind. When he stood up, he saw no trace of the eidos.

4

The crater smoked. Nene cautiously looked into the depression, then she turned back around after a bit.

"It feels so weird... Did the Founder really save us?"

"Basically. I don't know if she really meant to." Jhin sat on some debris.

Next to him, Sisbell was also perched on other rubble as though it were a chair as she stared at Mismis, who was on her side.

CHAPTER 3

"Sisbell, how's the commander?"

"You don't need to worry, Iska. She's in shock, which is very normal for people who have awakened as mages. But it is a little unusual for someone to fall unconscious so suddenly."

"I see…"

He let go of a sigh that had been waiting in his lungs. The nerves he'd had since coming to the eighth checkpoint had finally subsided slightly. The women farther off likely felt similarly.

"Lady Alice, I may be late in asking this, but why are you here?"

"Rin, you should start out by asking, *Are you all right?* before anything else, considering you're my attendant. By the way, I'm completely fine."

"I knew you'd say that, so I simply skipped the question."

Alice patted the dust off her clothes. Rin, who stood behind her, seemed somewhat glum. "Didn't you want me to stay in the Empire, Lady Alice?"

"I was worried about you. The Founder awakened and was going to attack the Empire. So I left the palace. But what's going on…?"

Alice gave the two symbols of the Empire and the Sovereignty, who were standing with their backs against the fencing, a dubious look.

"I thought you were just going to stand back and watch?"

"The whole thing was an eyesore."

"So have you rethought destroying the Empire?"

"I still plan to do it."

"But the villains in the Empire might have disappeared. I'll wait at the Lord's office, so come and see me to talk."

"You think I would really fall for that?"

"You don't have anything better to do anyway."

She had a hard time simply accepting it. Lord Yunmelngen

and the Founder Nebulis, who were supposed to be sworn enemies, were having a conversation as though they were friends. Undoubtedly, Alice didn't understand what was happening.

……Right, Alice is the only one who doesn't know how they're acquainted.

……We saw what happened a hundred years ago using Sisbell's Illumination.

The Founder and the Lord were old acquaintances. However, they had parted ways a hundred years ago. Alice was likely watching them with apprehension because she thought they were enemies who could start fighting at any moment.

"Seems like a waste of time…," the suntanned girl said bluntly. She got up from the fence. "Yunmelngen, I won't forgive the Empire for what it's done. However…"

"However? What?"

"It seems I have an opponent I need to crush before the Empire. I'll go prepare."

She turned around, her back facing Lord Yunmelngen. In that one moment, Iska thought he saw her glance his way.

"I hate this place. I don't want to be here."

She was acting like a sullen child. After making her feelings clear, the Founder Nebulis disappeared through a space rift.

INTERMISSION

The Covered Moon and Clouded Sun

1

She was left with a sense of foreboding.

The previous moonless night had made her chest squeeze tightly and chills run through her.

"Annihilated? What do you even mean?"

She only had a little farther to go on the highway that cut across the continent.

In just less than an hour more of driving, she saw the Imperial checkpoint. She abruptly stopped the wagon in the middle of it, then dashed out from the driver's seat.

Imperial territory, eighth checkpoint.

She looked up in the direction she was headed and gulped.

"Wait?! Lord Mask and Lady Kissing were there, and the forces were wiped out… What do you mean?!"

"We're still collecting information…"

She was corresponding with the Zoa intelligence unit. While Shanorotte had left for the Empire, another unit stayed behind at the Moon Spire and watched the movements of the Lou and Hydra.

"We have lost communication with Lord Mask and the fifteen from the elite unit with him. We can't get in touch with any of them."

"This can't be true…"

A cold sweat broke out on her forehead. She couldn't believe it. The news was so unimaginable that her throat tightened, and her voice grew hoarse.

"B-but the Revered Founder is headed to the Imperial capital, isn't she?! That was the whole reason why we decided now was the time to launch a surprise attack on the capital and free our captured brethren…"

"That was the plan."

"And Lady Kissing was there, too! Even if the Imperial forces had sent out a Saint Disciple, they couldn't have killed everyone!"

"That's why we have no idea what's going on, either!"

She heard a yell through the comm. On the other side of the line, she also heard someone hit a table.

"Shanorotte…go to the eighth checkpoint as planned."

"And then?"

"If the elite unit was annihilated, you should see traces of the aftermath. Gather all the intel you can. Also…there is still a remote chance that they simply had malfunctioning comms and couldn't get in touch with us."

"And if that isn't the case…?"

If it was true—if Lord Mask and Kissing and all the people they brought with them had been killed, what was she to do?

"_____"

The other end of the line was silent.

"Lord Growley, our leader, went missing during the Imperial forces' palace raid. And Lord Mask took leadership as the proxy while the Zoa household was shaken by our head's absence. The commanding officers, staff officers, and astral corps itself have their trust in him, and the Zoa household is currently centered around Lord Mask's abilities."

"That's right."

"And Lady Kissing is the Zoa's special weapon. The Lou's Aliceliese and the Hydra's Mizerhyby... Only Lady Kissing could compete against them in the conclave."

"So what? I'm asking you what's going to happen. What happens if we've lost Lord Mask and Lady Kissing?!"

"____"

The silence this time was longer. She had no idea how long she waited. Eventually, she heard a sigh of resignation from the other end of the line.

"Then the Zoa are as good as done."

"...Huh?!"

Then she heard a thud, and the line went dead as she realized the comm had been thrown on the ground.

"This can't be real... I should be the one throwing my comm down!"

Her thoughts were still in disarray. Her mind hadn't been able to keep up with reality, and even she realized that she was blanking out. If she attempted to drive again in this state, she was certain to crash.

"What is happening...?"

She balled her hand into a fist. Shanorotte felt the pain of her fingernails digging into the palm of her hand, and she gritted her teeth.

"The end of the Zoa? I'd never accept that! Never!"

If—and *only* if—that happened, she'd take everyone down, too. She'd go out with a bang.

2

The Nebulis royal palace.
Sun Spire terrace, bathed in bright morning light.

"Really now…the Lou and Zoa… We do not want to sink along with them."

He was Talisman, the head of the Hydra and known as "the Surge."

He wore a pure-white formal suit. His deep, chiseled features and dull golden hair made him a perfect male specimen at the age of forty.

However…

The man's commanding visage at that moment was grimly contorted in a way no person had witnessed before.

"We lost contact with the Eight Great Apostles. And the moment the Zoa family's unit reached the Imperial border, they were annihilated by some unknown force as well as the Imperial soldiers that were stationed there. Well then, Mizy."

"Yes, dearest Uncle," the princess sitting across from him answered.

Mizerhyby Hydra Nebulis IX.

The girl had a chiseled, deep-set face, and her hair was a stunning lapis lazuli. Though her hair had originally been as golden as Talisman's, the manifestation of her formidable astral power had transformed it blue. As the next in line to lead the Hydra, she was also their candidate for queen.

"I'll keep this brief. Would you be capable of doing this?" Talisman asked.

"No."

"Would Alice?"

"No."

She answered without hesitation, and she shook her head both times. "The Eight Great Apostles were the supreme authority pulling the strings behind the scenes in the Empire. She was able to wipe them out in a mere few hours and annihilate both the Zoa's and the Imperial forces without any survivors... What kind of person could do something so heartless and requiring so much power? This goes beyond human capabilities."

"Yes, you're right. I think you've made the correct determination."

Talisman touched his coffee cup; however, he did not pick it up. That was how deeply immersed he was in his thoughts.

"Human beings shouldn't possess the calamitous power at the planet's core, but among the several hundred subjects, only Elletear was able to adapt to it."

"That was what Kelvina summarized in her report."

However, what they meant by *adapt* was that the subject's body did not fall apart. They had expected Elletear's psyche to break under the strain of the great power and that they would be able to control her as part of their schemes. That was why the Eight Great Apostles had agreed to the experiment.

They had expected to gain a powerful doll.

But they had been wrong.

Instead, they'd created a true witch.

"We expected the power to swallow her... I can't believe she would be the one in control." He sighed.

Talisman wondered how long it had been since he had truly sighed after taking over as head of house.

INTERMISSION

"It's also been a while since I felt this irritated. Nothing has been going to plan. What do you make of it, Vichyssoise?"

"Right... Kinda sounds to me like this is a pretty bad situation to be in."

That was the third person on the terrace involved in their discussion. The red-haired girl leaned against the terrace's handrail. She wore a stud on her right ear and a hoop earring on her left. Though her combative eyes said she was a ruffian, this girl was no human—she was Subject Vi.

In the past, she had been taken to the same facility as Elletear.

"You truly believe it has come that far, even as someone in the same position as Elletear?"

"Oh, please don't, sir. I was a failure. If you compare Elletear and me, you'll end up making the same mistake as the Apostles."

"I would appreciate any advice you have to avoid their fate."

"I'm afraid I've got nothing. To put it simply, she's turned into an unstoppable monster. If we're careless, we might be wiped out, too." She was telling them to give up—the girl shrugged as if to drive that point home. "This may sound contradictory, but if we want to do anything, we need to act now."

"And what do you mean by that?"

"Elletear will continue to evolve."

"..."

"She'll likely head to the planet's core to get more of the calamity's power. And once that happens, it's game over. The Empire and Sovereignty would fall overnight."

"I see. So you mean that because she will only grow stronger, she is at her weakest now." The head of house crossed his arms. As Mizerhyby and Vichyssoise watched him, he silently continued to brood. "It seems the Eight Great Apostles have given birth to an unthinkable monstrosity."

He sighed again, then stood up. "Vichyssoise, do you know where Elletear is?"

"Hmm...it's just like I said. She'll aim to make contact with the calamity at the planet's core. And there's only one way to get there from the surface."

"A vortex, then?" Mizerhyby asked.

Following Talisman's lead, she stood up from her seat on the terrace bathed in sunlight.

"She'll look for an untouched vortex and trace it back to the core. A human could never do that, but Elletear might. Isn't that right, Uncle?"

"We should look into how we'll pursue her as quickly as possible."

Talisman turned around.

With the princess and his subordinate following him, the head of the house of sun left the dazzling terrace behind him.

However...none of them noticed it—that, as they had been mulling over their thoughts, the sun above them had been covered by clouds.

The very same dark clouds that had swallowed the stars and moon the night before were presently blotting out the sun, but not a single person from the Hydra family had noticed.

CHAPTER 4

More Than a Prisoner, Less Than a Guest

Imperial territory, eighth checkpoint.

When the Imperial forces' reinforcements arrived, the place looked like the scene of a disaster. The roads were split, railcars had been upended like cast-aside toys, the grass had been singed into char, and most conspicuous of all was the gigantic crater in the middle of the checkpoint.

"Can we really say the Founder did all this? Are you sure, Ms. Saint Disciple?"

"It's fine, Jhin-Jhin. His Excellency has said so. Oh…you there, medic, take the injured to get treatment. We'll ride a separate helicopter, so you don't have to wait for us."

Jhin scowled, but Risya kept up her easygoing tone. "If we come out to the public about the monster Elletear has become, we'll just have nothing but more trouble on our hands."

"I suppose you're right… And I guess the Eight Great Apostles were also the reason why she ended up like that."

"That's correct. The people responsible for it are gone, too."

That was why they were pinning it all on the Founder. It was true that the Founder Nebulis had attacked the seventh checkpoint nearby, and many people from the forces had witnessed it, too. That would be the simplest public announcement to make to the world.

"You, from the second communication team, once you get in touch with headquarters, make sure to—"

"Risya."

Risya was busily giving orders when Iska called out to her from behind.

"May I ask a question? It's nothing important, but…"

"Hmm? What's up, Isk?"

"I don't see the Lord or my master."

"The Lord went back ahead of us. Just think of what they look like. And after your master spoke with the Lord before they left, he wandered off somewhere, too."

"Why does he have to be so erratic?!"

He had a mountain of questions for his teacher. He understood most of what had taken place a century ago in the Empire through Sisbell's powers, but there was still something important that remained.

……*What is the calamity at the planet's core?*

……*And my master wasn't the only one who was concerned about it—the Founder and Elletear were, too.*

No one had told Iska what it was.

He'd learned only bits and pieces from his master and the Founder Nebulis's conversation. And that the swords in his hands were their hope to fight against the calamity.

"Hey, staff officer."

Rin had finished treating the wounds. Behind her, Alice was headed in their direction as well.

"There's something I want to check."

CHAPTER 4

"Ask away—as long as it's not about Imperial secrets or my age or weight, that is."

"It's about what's happening to them." Rin motioned with her chin at the Zoa's astral corps that the Imperial reinforcements were carrying.

......*Did they try to take advantage of the Founder's movements to get into the Empire?*

......*Then they ran into Elletear.*

They had likely been Elletear's next prey after the Eight Great Apostles, but they'd been wiped out simply upon meeting her.

Though he pitied them for running into an unreasonable battle against an indomitable opponent, he strangely also felt they'd gotten their just deserts.

"The Zoa family's decision ran counter to what our queen sought. Now that they've been captured by the Imperial forces, we don't plan to beg you to treat them with mercy. However, if you're planning any inhumane—"

"Oh, so that was what you were worried about." Risya dismissively waved her hand.

The medic team continued to carry away the comatose Zoa.

"They're headed to an astral-illness research institute. Chief Newton is such an astral-power maniac that he'll investigate whatever ails them regardless of whether they're friend or foe, especially considering that the illness is such a rarity... He'll treat them with care."

"And there better not be a change of plans for their treatment."

"All right, all right. Oh...? Looks like while we were talking, our helicopter arrived."

Risya looked up at the sky. It was a large aircraft, and one Iska was familiar with. It steadily descended. They would ride this helicopter back to the capital.

"It looks like this is good-bye, Iska."

When he turned around, he found a princess whose strawberry-blond hair fluttered in the wind looking up at him with a fleeting smile that seemed as though it could fall apart at any moment.

"We will leave through the border and go back to the Sovereignty. Mother must be worried about us, and most importantly, we need to tell her about Elletear."

"Oh, right..."

Yes. They had agreed to be Sisbell's guard only at the start. He never could have imagined their contract in Alsamira would have led to such a long journey.

"Is Commander Mismis still unconscious?"

"She's awake now. Nene and Jhin are keeping an eye on her, so you don't have to worry."

"Please thank the three of them for me as well. You too, Rin."

"Excuse me?"

When Sisbell said the attendant's name, Rin blinked in surprise.

"You should thank them, too."

"Me?! Why?!"

"It seemed to me like the Lord was catering to your every need in that room. You had such lavish meals each day."

"I was a prisoner, you realize?! A-anyway, it was all a misunderstanding! They never showed me any hospitality at all!" Rin insisted, her face going red.

"Lady Alice, Lady Alice, please say something!"

"____"

"......Lady Alice?"

Rin felt something was off and turned around. Beside her, the golden-haired girl was silently staring at the ground. It seemed she hadn't listened to Sisbell and Rin's conversation at all.

CHAPTER 4

"Alice?"

"Huh?"

The moment Iska said her name, she jumped in surprise and let out a small yelp despite not responding to anyone else until that moment.

"Wh-what?! You... Why would you shout at me suddenly like that...?"

"I wasn't the only one. Rin was, too. She was calling your name."

"What?"

"Hmm..." Rin's eyes suddenly grew cold. "You won't respond to me, but you will to the Imperial swordsman, then?"

"Of course not! It was a coincidence... I just had something on my mind!"

Alice suddenly flipped her golden hair. Even though she was acting strong at the moment, he felt as though he saw something fragile about her from her side profile, but Iska wrote it off as having been his imagination.

"Let's go back to the Sovereignty... Shall we, Rin? Sisbell?"

Alice turned around—or so Iska thought. She seemed to linger for a few seconds as though hesitating about something; then the Nebulis princess turned her clear face partially toward him.

"Iska...I can't talk to you much, considering our positions, but it seems I owe you after this. Thank you for watching over Rin and my sister."

"It's just how things panned out. I merely chose to do what I needed to in order to survive."

"......Yes, of course."

She suddenly smiled. Then she turned to face the checkpoint's gate.

"Oh, wait right there."

* * *

A voice came from Risya's comm. It was the Lord's voice—the very one who had disappeared not too long ago.

"Oh, Lord? Didn't you already go back?"

"I'm in the Lord's office. Anyway, Risya, are the Sovereign princesses still there? Princess Aliceliese in particular."

"Me...?" Alice turned around, looking nervous. "Did the leader of the Empire just say my name?"

"Don't you want to know what happened to your older sister to make her like that?"

"...Huh?" Alice gulped. She'd been planning on not letting anything perturb her, but she found it hard not to react to this. "Then let me ask you a question. How much do you know?"

"More than you would. After all, I do look the way I do. I'm a monster much in the same way as your sister."

"H-how dare you call her that...!"

"A monster? Just look around you. All the Imperial forces and astral corps who are being carried behind you were victims of Elletear. She didn't make a distinction between them. Or does this look like anything other than an act of savagery to you?"

"...W-well..." Alice wasn't sure what to say. She understood that Elletear was no longer the sister she had known.

"It'll be worth your while. I'll tell you all I know about that monster. So come back with Risya."

"Huh?!"

"What?!"

Sisbell reacted first, then Rin. Simply put, the Lord was saying that they wouldn't be returning to the Sovereignty. Alice was being called to the Lord's office—in other words, the capital.

"Are you asking me to become a prisoner of the Empire?"

"I suppose you're more than a prisoner but not quite a

CHAPTER 4

guest." There was a nonchalant laugh from the other end of the line. "That's right, Princess Aliceliese. You're the Ice Calamity Witch, aren't you?"

"..." Alice didn't say anything. The Ice Calamity Witch was feared and reviled by the Imperial forces. Confirming his suspicions was possibly very dangerous.

As though the Lord had seen through Alice's conflicted emotions, the beastperson said, "**No hard feelings, just for now.**"

The voice on the other end of the line was incredibly calm. In fact, even Iska felt it was surprisingly anticlimactic listening to the indifferent tone from beside them.

"**As long as you promise not to make a ruckus, I won't do anything uncalled-for, either. And I promise you as much freedom as you want.**"

"What are you plotting...?"

"**This conversation will serve in my self-interest as well.**"

In that moment, they all imagined the beastperson flashing a smile full of fangs.

"**I'd like you to defeat your own sister.**"

A war between siblings.

The Lord had proposed a ghastly future for the sisters.

"**I came up with the idea based on the earlier conversation. It seems Elletear hasn't been able to fully abandon her love for her own family. So wouldn't you be the most ideal assassin? I'll give you all the information you need to know in order to defeat her.**"

The Lord's proposal showed no restraint. Who knows how long it must have taken the Lord to come up with such a plan. Alice took the comm and offered up a weak, wan smile.

"What more would I expect from the Empire? You truly show no mercy to witches."

"**Your sister is planning to destroy your home country soon, you know?**"

"———"

"**We're already past the point where we can think of only protecting our own countries. Either we both survive or we all go down together. If you don't want to cooperate, you can go home. You're free to wait for your fate in your home country.**"

"I'll..."

She went silent again. Alice hung her head and was quiet as everyone's gazes were on her.

"I—"

But in the moment of Alice's much-awaited decision, the girl with strawberry-blond hair interjected. "Th-then I'll stay!"

"**Oh? Was that Princess Sisbell I heard?**"

"It is I!" Sisbell placed a hand on her breast. "Elletear is no longer herself... No, perhaps that was who she always was, but if that's the case, as her sister, I need to stop her!"

"**Oh?**" The Lord seemed rather amused. "**But your astral powers aren't suited for battle. Do you plan on heading straight to your death, then?**"

"I can help in other ways instead of fighting. And I think more than anyone else in the Sovereignty, the best person to consult on how to stop Elletear is you."

"**How clever you are. You've understood correctly.**"

"And don't you still need my abilities? I should be able to help with analyzing my sister's powers."

"**I applaud your nobility, unlike a certain half-hearted second princess.**"

"Why, of course!" The third princess thrust out her chest as though it was her time to shine. "In place of my cowardly sister Alice, I will— Mrf!"

"Wh-wh-who's supposed to be cowardly?!"

This time it was Alice's turn. Just as her younger sister was triumphantly making her declaration, Alice had placed both her hands on either side of her sister's face and squeezed her cheeks, and she seemed to glare at her sister as though challenging her.

"Unlike you, I think through my decisions!"

"Hee-hee. Are you scared, Sister?"

"Of course I'm not! Ugh, fine then." Alice let out a long sigh. She exchanged looks with Rin, then glared at the comm in her hand. "You can take us anywhere you want in the Empire. But you must treat us courteously. If you don't, I *will* go on a full rampage."

INTERMISSION

The Bent and Abandoned Thorn

1

Imperial capital, third military hospital.

This was the sole hospital within the Empire that specialized in astral diseases. Though very few could use Curse, Brainwash, and Poison astral powers, that also made treating such afflictions exceedingly difficult. And because of that, the doctors at this hospital were all experts in treating astral illnesses.

The hospital's second ward.

"Well, looks like we're gonna get busy. This is an astral illness we've never seen before, after all."

The hallway was bathed in bluish-white light.

The cheerful voice echoed through the milk-white tiled hallway as a thin man briskly walked down the hall. His assistant wearing a white coat accompanied him by his side.

"It's the eighth checkpoint. We believe the incident occurred about seven hours ago. Is that right, Michaela?"

"Yes."

"Thirty-nine victims in total. Twenty Imperial soldiers who were guarding the checkpoint. And nineteen elite Nebulis forces that were trying to invade Imperial territory. All of them were taken down. Their common symptom is a coma caused by some unknown factor. They have been unable to regain consciousness. So what's been tried thus far?"

"Noises, including calling their names. External physical stimuli, such as hitting their shoulders. Strong stimulants. None had any effect."

"All right." The emaciated man nodded in satisfaction once Michaela, the medical professional, had finished her smooth delivery of the report. "Michaela, the chart, if you could?"

"Chief Newton."

"What is it?"

"You already have the chart in your hand."

"Oh my. It seems you're right. I was so lost in thought, I'd forgotten. It's like when you're wearing your own glasses while looking for them."

When Michaela pointed that out, the bearded chief smiled wryly. The Saint Disciple of the tenth seat was Sir Karossos Newton, the laboratory's chief.

His nickname was the "sickliest researcher." The man's shoulders and limbs looked as though they would snap with a light breeze. They showed he was an exception—he was the only civil official among the greatest military force called the Saint Disciples.

"Do you think the one who did this is the Founder Nebulis?"

"That is what will be reported to the public. We received word from Ms. Risya that the truth is one of the Eight Great Apostles' secret experiments went rogue. So in more concrete terms, it means the Nebulis Sovereignty's First Princess Elletear was the one who did this."

INTERMISSION

"A witch of yet-unknown capacity, then...," Chief Newton murmured quietly. "That does seem to align with the astral illness we are dealing with this time. We haven't seen any precedent for it. The Eight Great Apostles were likely trying to investigate whether they could create a witch greater than the one we already know exists. The thirty-nine at the eighth checkpoint were simply unlucky they were attacked. Though they're also lucky to be alive."

"You consider *this* lucky?"

"Of course. I can examine them, do my research, and help them recover—that is what I intend to do, at least."

He flung out his arms and almost sang the words. That man stopped at a room at the end of the hall.

"Especially her. She is the only witness who has faced the witch Elletear and lived to tell the tale. Well...I suppose all thirty-nine survived, but she is the only one who can speak."

"Please be careful," Michaela said. She already had a gun holster conspicuously hanging off her hip. "She's a purebred type. She may look like a young girl, but Ms. Risya has said she's as dangerous and powerful in combat as the Ice Calamity Witch."

"How exciting. Wonderful."

"She's in three different astral-sealing handcuffs...but we don't know how well those will hold back her purebred powers. We're keeping an eye on her with surveillance cameras, and I've requested she be shot if she shows any sign of hostility or abnormality."

"What is the witch's name?"

"According to the report..." Michaela scanned the paper in her hand.

"It's Kissing."

* * *

The door unlocked. It creaked solemnly as its massive metal facade swung open.

It was a witch interrogation room. It was furnished with a rectangular table and two nondescript chairs. The ceiling was equipped with three cameras. In addition, astral-energy sensors were installed in the corners of the ceiling and floor.

"Pardon me, my lovely girl."

Chief Newton and Michaela entered.

A black-haired girl sat in one chair and did not so much as flinch. Her face was charming, and though small, her lips were a fine bloodred color. If someone were to pass by her on the street, they likely would have turned to take another glance at her beautiful features.

However...

She continued to stare at the ground, and she did not react to the two doctors in the slightest as they walked in.

"How are you feeling? We need to keep the handcuffs on you for our own safety, but if you have any requests other than to have those off, please tell me."

"____"

"And please don't worry, my dear. We do not intend you any harm. Well, I suppose that may sound cliché. I won't deny it's a classic line that would be used to win someone over."

"____"

"Well, let's cut to the chase, shall we? We—the Empire, I mean to say—would like to work with you."

Newton took a seat. He faced Kissing across the table.

"You were attempting to cross into Imperial territory. As you approached the eighth checkpoint, you had the misfortune of encountering a monster. Isn't that right?"

"Guh." She flinched. Chief Newton didn't fail to notice the slight shudder.

INTERMISSION

She was frightened.

The monster had left a deep mark on the psyche of a purebred type who made the Imperial forces shudder herself.

"I know you saw the monster's power."

"____"

"We are looking for information. We need clues in order to treat those who have fallen prey to her. That includes your fellow astral-corps members, of course."

"My...fel...low...?"

This was the first time the girl had spoken.

"My uncle...?"

"Hmm? Who's this uncle of yours?"

"____"

"Oh, pardon me. It seems you don't want me to pry."

Chief Newton dramatically cleared his throat. A few seconds passed.

"Now, I know you may have some reservations about working with the Imperial forces, but it truly isn't a big deal at all."

"____"

"This is a trade—a strategic negotiation of mutual benefit, if you will. We are simply making a transaction that will help us both. You give us information about the witch's secrets that you witnessed, and we will use that to research a method to wake the victims up from their comas. That means your fellow companions will awaken, too. Now, isn't that a happy thing for us both?"

"____"

The girl remained silent.

Though she had shown fear for a moment and temporarily broken her silence, that was like nothing more than the ripple of water in a fountain. The water would reclaim its serenity in the same way the girl's face immediately grew clouded over in deep shadow.

She had no intention of talking to him.

No. Her will to talk had been eroded away—that was the impression she gave.

"Hey, hey, hey, hey!"

Right at that moment, there was a commotion and the sound of footsteps.

"I'm coming in, Newt!"

The door was theatrically kicked open, and a wild-looking female soldier came rushing in.

This was the Saint Disciple of the third seat, the Incessant Tempest, Mei. She had messy long hair and tanned skin, as well as bizarrely long canines that peeked out from her lips.

She wore a combat-uniform-style tank top from which her arms of steel protruded. The gleam in her eyes gave her the look of a large feline predator.

Right then, her eyes flashed.

"Newt, you really caught that witch?!"

"Hmm? How unusual. Why would you leave your post guarding His Excellency to come to a gloomy place like this?"

"Out of curiosity, obviously. And I came here to horse around a little."

She triumphantly entered the interrogation room. Then she looked down at the handcuffed girl seated at the table and let out a "wow!"

"I am Kissing Zoa Nebulis IX."

"My nickname's the Incessant Tempest. I'll teach you why I'm called that."

They'd fought to kill each other in the past when the Imperial forces tried to attack the Nebulis palace as part of an operation. Mei had headed to the Moon Spire and begun a battle with Kissing.

INTERMISSION

At the time, they'd concluded in a draw.

"Wow, what a surprise. It's really her. How'd you catch her?"

The Saint Disciple peered at the witch who was her sworn enemy.

"Been a while, missy. Too bad we were interrupted back then. Wait, didja really get yourself captured before we could even settle things? Or what? Did you let yourself get caught just so you could see me?"

"____"

The young witch still did not respond. She remained silent and continued to look down. Mei didn't seem worried and simply drew her face close out of curiosity.

"Hey, c'mon, answer me, will you? You can still use your astral powers even with those handcuffs on, can't you? Unlike those guys, I can tell. Stop pretending to comply and attack already. C'mon."

"____"

"Heeey, missy. You still waiting for something?"

Mei leaned forward.

She playfully looked at the witch's face, which was still downcast. However…Newton and Michaela could see Mei's face cloud soon after. At first, she'd seemed curious, but then her expression steadily turned sour. And finally…

Whoom!

She suddenly threw the table right into the ceiling.

"Eep!" Michaela screamed and cowered. "Wh-wh-what do you think you're doing, Ms. Mei?! Why would you destroy a table?!"

"'Cause I'm frustrated."

The table had turned into splinters when Mei had kicked it while righting herself. The wreckage flitted through the air and fell on Michaela's and Newton's heads.

"Boring…," Mei grumbled.

The black-haired girl still hadn't so much as flinched despite the destruction. Mei looked down at her soberly.

"She's been completely broken."

"Hmm?"

"Yeah, Newt, questioning her is meaningless. There's nothing left in there. She's just a husk that's lost all her spirit and willpower... Ugh, why'd I even bother coming?"

She let out a dramatic sigh.

"There's no point in even provoking her. See ya, Newt. I'm leaving her to you."

She turned her back on them without waiting for a reply.

There was something despondent about her footfalls as the Saint Disciple of the third seat disappeared down the hall.

Fifteen minutes had passed since then.

After the witch had remained silent no matter how they addressed her, both Newton and Michaela had also given up on negotiating and left the room.

2

Night fell.

The curtain of black smoothly descended upon the bright blue skies, reaching the horizon. Now was time for the moon to shine brightly. She had been taught as a child that night was nothing to be frightened of. The radiant moon in the night sky was sure to keep her safe.

They were the family under the moon's protection. That was what she had been taught about the Zoa family and what she had grown up to believe.

INTERMISSION

......But now what will I do?
......I can't believe that anymore. Even if I want to, I'm so scared of the night that I can't.
And it was all *that* person's fault.

"I will let you listen to the requiem of the planet."

"Guh."

Her entire body shuddered; then Kissing was struck with full-body shivers.

She'd recalled it all over again. The Lou family's First Princess Elletear... The sound of the monster's voice. She could tell through her special eyes—unique eyes that contained her astral crest—she could see the flow of astral energy.

The Revered Founder: Greater than anyone else's. Ferocious. A storm.

The Lord: Small but magnificent. An extensive mountain.

Aliceliese: Large. Beautiful. An ice flower.

Mizerhyby: Large. Brilliant. The sun.

Sisbell: Small. Fleeting. Fluorescent.

And the astral corps: Very small. Each slightly different.

But hers was bad. The power surging from Elletear's entire body had transformed into something that was no longer astral energy.

It was something absolutely wicked.

The closest she could describe it was as a reaper, as a nightmare. Simply seeing it had made her feel the specter of death.

However...

She was still alive.

Why?

Was it because she was strong? It wasn't that.

Had she been saved by someone else?

Had Elletear let her go?

No.

She'd been protected.

"Uncle…"

The floor was cold.

She crawled along the nearly pitch-black room. On a bed in the corner of the room was a man on a respirator.

He had a large burn mark on the right side of his face.

She'd been told it was from a wound he'd suffered while young in a battle against the Imperial forces. It was painful to look at, and so, as a member of the royal family and someone who was very visible to the public eye, he had covered it with an extravagant mask. And out of a sense of satire, he had begun to go by another name after that—Lord Mask.

Now his face was bare. Showing it to the Imperial forces was likely a humiliation he would have died rather than have happen. But without taking it off, he could not be on the respirator.

"Uncle…"

She caressed his scar. She imagined him waking up—*Stop that, Kissing*, he'd say—but he didn't. She knew such a vain hope was too convenient to come true.

He wouldn't open his eyes.

In that moment, all the Zoa's elite forces present at the checkpoint should have been incapacitated.

But…

"I will let you listen to the requiem of the planet."
"Run, Kissing! You have to—"

Lord Mask On's astral power was Gate.

Before the witch Elletear could use her Planet's Requiem, a

teleportation gate had opened in front of Kissing. And then everything had gone dark…

Before she realized it, she was alone and far away from everyone else, and they had all fallen over.

"…Uh…why…?" She began to sob. "Uncle…Uncle…you could have escaped, too, couldn't you…?"

One person could escape—he could have escaped on his own.

"You did this to save me… You sacrificed yourself…"

Noon had passed; then night arrived.

Even if she waited until morning, she knew he wouldn't wake. Not ever.

"I'm sorry!"

The dam broke.

In the hazy light, the beautiful girl's eyes welled with giant tears that began to fall.

"I'm sorry… I'm sorry, I'm sorry, sorry, sorry… I—I was too weak! It must have hurt. You must still be hurting…but I…I can't do anything!"

She realized she was powerless.

She had been applauded for her wonderful powers. She'd been lionized as someone fit to be queen, but she was painfully aware of just how weak she was.

And…

She had understood one other thing.

"Uncle…I realized…that something as frightening as this could exist…"

Was it the monster?

The fear from facing death?

No, not those.

"I'm afraid…of being alone…"

Lord Mask remained on the bed. No matter how she called him or caressed his scar, he did not wake. He could no longer say her name. And he would not pat her head anymore.

The moment she realized that, she understood. More than the despair of not being able to defeat the witch Elletear, more than the fear of facing death…

"I'm frightened of being alone. I don't want a world without you, Uncle…"

More than death and more than anything, she feared the thought of being alone forever.

"You may be upset with me, Uncle…"

She held the hand of the man who had lost his mask. With her trembling hands, she gripped his.

"I do not have the option to choose. No matter what I need to do…I will get revenge for you."

The dark clouds parted.

In the observation room, under the piercing moonlight, the princess of the moon lifted her face.

CHAPTER 5

The Relationship Alice Knew Not Of

1

Inside the transport helicopter.

In the airlift heading to the capital, Risya signaled Unit 907 to come closer with her hand.

"Mismis, Isk, Jhin-Jhin, and Nene. I have something important to talk about, so come here for a sec."

"Now, this doesn't bode well." Jhin was the first to stand up. "I've never heard you call anything *important to talk about* before. You were even blunt about how the Lord looks... So this has got to be something bad, hasn't it?"

"That's right. I'll just preface it by saying it's something very bad." Risya shrugged. Even her usual carefree gesture seemed to have a bothered air around it. "Let me ask you this, Mismis: How bad do you think the damage Elletear dealt the Empire is?"

"What? Um..." Commander Mismis began to deliberate. "The Eight Great Apostles in charge of the Imperial assembly are gone...so the Empire's upper management is in chaos, I guess?"

"Correct. You got one thing right."

"And she took out the troops stationed at the eighth checkpoint, so that must have hurt the Imperial forces."

"That's half right."

"......Huh?"

"It doesn't just hurt—it's a heavy loss. Calling it *enormous* wouldn't even be an exaggeration. It was enough to make the Lord return to the capital immediately."

From the helicopter window, Risya looked down at the Empire's streets.

"Next I'll ask you, Isk."

"Ask me what?"

"Elletear fought with the Apostles in the Imperial assembly five thousand meters underground. You saw that using Princess Sisbell's Illumination power, didn't you?"

"Yes."

"Did nothing about that bother you? For example, Elletear went five thousand meters underground. It isn't that odd that she got down there in itself since she isn't human, but just how did she do it?"

"Uh, from the surfa—"

He paused. He hadn't stopped intentionally. The moment he'd started to talk, a certain possibility had come to mind and made his throat tighten and his voice catch. In order to reach the Imperial assembly, she would have needed to go underground.

That was obvious.

......But think about it.

......What's right above the Imperial assembly?

He didn't even need to think any further. That was because whenever he was called by the Eight Great Apostles, he'd always gone to the Imperial forces' base.

CHAPTER 5

"The central base..."

"Yes. That's where you all did your training and where the assemblies were held. Elletear penetrated through that point. Do you think someone who plans to destroy both the Empire and the Sovereignty would just pass on through without doing anything at all?"

"..."

He felt sweat roll down his cheek. The image of what had happened at the eighth checkpoint came to mind even when he didn't want it to. To Elletear, the thousands of soldiers at the central base would have been nothing more than prey. If she came across them, she would have...

"Risya, you're joking, right?" Commander Mismis asked, her lips trembling. "You don't mean...even the central base's people were..."

"Twenty percent of them." Risya's response was as direct as could be. "When Elletear entered the base, about sixty percent of the personnel were there. The rest were out on missions like we are or were on business trips. So...only a few dozen soldiers went to intercept her, but they weren't the only ones caught up in the attack. We had collateral damage."

Elletear had used her as-yet-unidentified power. It must have spread throughout the base like a shock wave, dragging others down with it.

"They have the same symptoms. They're in a comatose state."

"Twenty percent of them?" Jhin sat back down in his seat and sighed deeply. "The commonly accepted theory is that once an organization loses thirty percent of its staff, it will cease to function. On the battlefield, it'd mean being wiped out. What do you make of losing twenty percent of the personnel, Ms. Saint Disciple?"

"We're right on the verge of mayhem and not being able to

function." Risya smiled wryly. There was an uncharacteristic impatience in her voice. "And of course, leaders and commanding officers were included in that twenty percent. The chain of command is nearly paralyzed. Well, what I'm really trying to say is don't be shocked when you see the state of the base."

And speak of the devil, as Risya looked down, the base came into view.

2

Central base.

When Iska first disembarked from the helicopter, he saw nothing unusual about the base.

It hadn't been destroyed, burned down, or damaged at all... He didn't see anything wrong with it externally. The outer wall was as good as pristine. The lawn and maneuvering grounds looked vibrant, and some flowers even bloomed in the nooks of the base.

What was different, however, was that the inside was practically deserted.

"They're busy with transporting and taking care of the comatose patients. The ones who aren't tied down are busy with communications and meetings. Anyone wandering outside the base is either shirking their duties or a Sovereign spy. Regardless of which they are, we'll need to capture them quickly."

"Is this really what it's come to...?"

Risya walked right onto the grounds. Iska walked next to her, studying their surroundings as he went. Normally, military cars would be driving busily along the roads, but even those were empty, as well as the sidewalks.

CHAPTER 5

"We're in quite a bit of trouble, considering the Eight Great Apostles were also taken out."

Risya gave a forced smile.

"They say fight fire with fire, right? Well, those villains were keeping others in line through fear. Now that the Eight Great Apostles are gone, the ambitious people in the assembly and criminals will probably go on the move. That might affect peace in the capital for a while."

"Risya, what does that mean…?"

"Hmm?"

"Think of the worst-case scenario, if the Nebulis Sovereignty attempts to lead a giant battle against us right now."

"Well, then we'd be in a huge emergency. Even if they didn't manage to bring down the capital, they might still grab some of the other major cities."

That was no exaggeration, either. The upper echelons of the Empire were in shambles. With how many casualties the Imperial forces already had, they needed to avoid a battle with the Sovereignty.

"Isk, you probably have already guessed, but that's part of the reason why the Lord wanted the witch sisters to stay here in the capital."

"They probably understand that, too…"

Alice and Sisbell were both princesses. In other words, the Sovereignty wouldn't be able to make any thoughtless moves while they were here.

"They're kind of dangerous hostages, all things considered…"

"That's why I'm leaving them in your care, Isk."

Risya walked onto the grass.

"We really should have three Saint Disciples guarding those

two princesses, but they currently have their hands full helping headquarters reestablish chain of command. And the first seat decided to disappear on us. Figuring out what to do with the empty first seat was already an urgent issue. So anyway!"

Risya suddenly stopped.

She pointed at the Lord's office.

"The three witches are in the Lord's office, so keep an eye on them, Isk!"

"The Lord's office? Wouldn't it be bad if they went on a rampage there…?"

"Is there anywhere else we could hide them? If anyone finds out the Imperial forces took in witches from the Nebulis Sovereignty, it'd be a big deal."

"Well, you have a point…"

"So c'mon, go and keep them reined in to make sure they don't cause a ruckus."

She makes it sound so easy. Iska grumbled and sighed, then turned away from Risya.

It was often called the "windowless building." That was the Lord's office where Lord Yunmelngen lived as a recluse. They were at the entrance where they were meant to meet.

"Looks like the four of us are being transferred to Special Division I."

"Huh?" When that was the first thing Jhin said, Iska couldn't help but question it. "Jhin, say that again."

"As of this afternoon, Special Division III Unit 907 has been reassigned to Special Division I. If we stayed in Division III and kept coming in and out of the Lord's office, our colleagues would think something's up."

CHAPTER 5

"..."

"Did Ms. Saint Disciple not tell you? She proposed it."

"She didn't mention a thing about it."

Ha-ha. He let out a strained laugh before he realized it.

......I don't think she just forgot to tell me, either.

......She probably didn't say anything because she wanted it to come as a surprise.

Iska's unit was from Special Division III. They were a reinforcement unit normally deployed to remote regions from the Imperial capital to lend assistance. Their missions in the Nelka Woods and Mudor Canyon were case in point.

Division I, on the other hand, was the equivalent of the Imperial elite's secret service. Simply put, they were the cream of the crop, even among the elite units.

"And we're specifically the Lord's guard unit in Division I. That means we report to the Saint Disciples, not headquarters. We'll be able to enter the Lord's office freely this way."

"So Risya is our commanding officer?"

"That's right. It's basically getting a promotion in the Imperial forces, which is a surprise, to say the least. We weren't looking to get promoted, though."

Jhin brought their identification up to the door. With a blip, the door swung open to the Lord's office, which was unbelievable to watch already. This door couldn't be opened by anyone in Division III.

It seemed they were already officially in Division I.

"Is the commander inside?"

"She's at Imperial headquarters. She's gotta finish our transfer process in the next three hours, so Nene went with her to help, since she can't do it alone."

"Oh, so that's why the two of them aren't with you."

"So we just need to hang tight for two more hours. We're supposed to wait inside."

They headed into the Lord's office. They'd been in this building just hours before, but the circumstances were now different, and they were no longer Risya's guests. Now, they were here officially as the Lord's guards.

The hallway was deserted. No matter how far he looked down the several dozen meters of the hallway, he saw no one else walking around.

Clack…clack…

Only Iska's and Jhin's shoes echoed in the space. They didn't see any guards or office workers.

Or so they thought.

"Oh? I recognize you."

In the middle of the hall, they found a rather feral-looking female soldier sitting cross-legged. She was the Saint Disciple of the third seat, the Incessant Tempest, Mei. When Iska had once been the lowest seat of the Saint Disciples, she'd been his coworker.

"Mei, um, it's been a while."

"Say, Isk…"

When she looked at him, she sighed heavily. She seemed very dispirited.

"Kinda boring not having a rivalry going, am I right?"

"Excuse me?"

"Here's the report: I'm guarding the Lord's office with the second seat, and Risya is also in command. And you're going to be working for us…haaah…"

"Where's the second seat?"

"On standby outside the Lord's office. He hates witches more than I do. I know there were reasons for bringing them in, but he

CHAPTER 5

just wants to pummel them when he sees their faces. So he's been stationed outside under the Lord's orders. I'm on duty guarding the inside…haaah…"

He had to wonder how many times she'd already sighed.

"I'm really down in the dumps right now, though. Isk, this isn't your first time here, right? We'll skip the tour, then. Just head straight in."

"All right…"

Mei stayed seated and didn't so much as turn around. He continued down the glass skywalk ahead.

They were on the top floor of the four buildings, which was called the Heaven of Insight and Nonsight. When he set foot in that place, the pungent and strong scent of grass tickled his nose. They were in the Lord's chambers. The moment he took a step into the large hall, which was mostly red…

"Hey, Lord! What's the meaning of this?!" He heard Rin's voice echo all around. "You were the one who said the fourth-floor office would be converted into a bedroom for Lady Alice and Lady Sisbell!"

"That's right. And I said I'd leave everything to you as the one responsible for their accommodations." The Lord, who was lying on the floor, opened their eyes and appeared annoyed. **"You saw during the afternoon battle, didn't you? I'm feeling terrible, so let me sleep."**

"The closet I ordered for Lady Alice has yet to arrive!"

"It's being arranged for now." Then the Lord let out a large yawn. **"Do you understand? If you do, let me sleep…"**

"Lord! Lord! Where are my stuffed animals?!" Sisbell shouted.

She ran over to the silver-furred beastperson before they could close their eyes.

"I can't sleep without a stuffed animal. May I order one?!"

"**Do what you like...**"

"And a carpet and sofa as well?!"

"**I'm going to sleep...**"

"Oh! Hey, wait! I haven't finished yet!"

The beastperson curled up and went to sleep. As Jhin watched Sisbell shake the beastperson's shoulder, he murmured, "She's like a kid messing with her pet." Iska happened to fully agree.

"So what now, Iska?"

"What do you mean?"

"We need to keep an eye on those three. Looks like two of them are here, but where's the third one? What should we do about her? It doesn't seem like she'd do anything bad just because she doesn't have a guard on her, though."

"It's Princess Aliceliese; she's probably fine."

He'd almost called her Alice, but he didn't reveal to Jhin that he had almost used her nickname.

"But I'll go find her. I'll leave Rin and Sisbell with you," Iska said.

"Are you sure?"

"I don't think they'll cause trouble. If anything happens, tell me right away."

He watched from the corner of his eyes as Rin and Sisbell made a fuss.

Then Iska left the Lord's chamber.

3

Fourth floor of one building of the Lord's office.

In a corner of a large room labeled the "Jade Chamber," Alice crouched as she looked up silently at the ceiling.

CHAPTER 5

"…"

A sense of lethargy loomed over her.

Why was it? Why was she feeling a sense of loss she'd never felt before?

"I'll overthrow the Empire. Once I do that, I'll create a world where no one is persecuted."

She'd been dreaming of that this whole time. She'd believed overthrowing the Empire would mean the world would no longer persecute astral mages. But…

"If the Sovereignty did defeat the Empire, it would be thanks to the powerful mages."

"That would only serve to accelerate astral-power supremacism in the Nebulis Sovereignty. And the weak mages would have even less of a role."

The contradiction had been thrust before her.

The difference in how astral mages were treated lay in the shadows of the Sovereignty's promising form of "justice" to overthrow the Empire. The Sovereignty also oppressed astral mages in its own way, and overthrowing the Empire wouldn't change that fact—it would worsen it.

She had no response.

She didn't think her sister's argument entirely made sense, either. But for a moment, her heart had wavered. She hadn't been able to respond because she realized her sister might have been right in some ways.

She was mortified by that. She'd known from the past—she couldn't win against Elletear.

She was too smart. That applied to looks, grace, education, and even social skills.

Her sister had it all. In contrast, Alice's one and only saving grace—her astral power—was also something her sister had outpaced.

....

......*But really?*

Was that really what frustrated her?

It wasn't.

The thing that surprised her most was actually…

"You've always fought on your own."

"Alice, do you have a knight who would protect you?"

It was also her resourcefulness, her sensibility, her ideals. Alice felt there was a huge disparity between them, and her sister came out on top.

......*Am I alone?*

......*There's…no way.*

She wasn't alone. She had her mother, Rin, and followers who looked up to her.

But…

Her sister had told her that wasn't what she meant. Family and servants were entirely different from the knight her sister spoke of. In any time or age, knights would always protect the princess.

She didn't understand.

"Sister…what were you trying to say…?"

She hadn't ever thought of herself as someone needing protecting.

She was a princess, after all. She'd believed she was supposed to become stronger than anyone else so she could protect everyone—that was the ideal. That was why she'd wanted to become more powerful.

CHAPTER 5

But her resolve had been overturned from its foundations.

"You were too strong, so you fought alone."
"That's why you have no knight beside you. And that's the reason why you cannot win against me."

Her sister had someone. She had a Saint Disciple, the most powerful guard she could have. Alice didn't understand it, but the two seemed to be tied together by the unbelievably strong trust they had in each other.
......*If she can call that guard her knight...*
......*Then right now I...*
A strong power.
A strong knight.
Now that her sister had both, how could she stand up to Elletear?
"Huh!"
Tap.
When Alice suddenly heard a knock at the door, she flinched and raised her face. She expected it to be Rin or Sisbell. After Alice convinced herself of that, she chided herself internally only a moment later for letting down her guard, for the person who entered was the Imperial swordsman.
"Iska?"

He took a step into the room.
The bed and closet had yet to be brought in. Alice was inside the room in the middle of its remodeling while it was still virtually empty.

In the spacious room, she was crouching in a corner.

"Iska?"

Alice quickly stood up.

When Iska realized her eyes were red and swollen, he quickly started making excuses for coming in.

"Oh, no, it wasn't like that. Sorry, uh…I need to fulfill my duties, too…"

Had Alice been crying?

Thinking he'd seen something he shouldn't have, he found his sense of duty as a guard was quickly overcome by feelings of guilt for barging into a girl's room.

"Why are you apologizing?" Alice gave him a weak smile. She quickly wiped the red corners of her eyes. "This is Imperial territory. And it's where the Lord lives, isn't it? Of course they would give the Ice Calamity Witch a skilled guard."

"I'm glad I don't need to explain…"

"I understand the situation I'm in."

Alice sighed. Her earlier weakness was gone and had been replaced with her usual firm and charming gaze.

"The Lord promised that Rin and Sisbell would be safe. As long as that's true, I'll behave."

Alice wanted the Lord to tell her more about Elletear's transformation.

……*And how to defeat my sister.*

……*Because she's trying to destroy the Sovereignty.*

Alice would likely be here for several days. And during that time, Unit 907, which had transferred to Division I, would likely be keeping an eye on her. But there was one thing that still bothered Iska.

Why had Alice's eyes been red?

After some contemplation—but not too much to warrant

suspicion—Iska concluded it was because she felt humiliated as a princess to be captured by the Empire.

……*Alice has her pride as a Sovereign princess.*

……*And she was captured by the Empire. Of course she's upset—she's like a bird in a cage.*

Iska assumed this had to be the reason.

"His Excellency and Risya said this, too."

He turned to face Alice and did his best to put together his next words.

"We're treating you as a guest. So, um…don't be upset."

"____"

Alice was silent. But then she suddenly grinned and laughed.

"Is that your way of being considerate?"

"What? No, I…"

"It's not that." Her voice quivered slightly. Her gaze dropped to the floor. "My sister said that I'm alone."

"Alone? What's that supposed to mean? What about Rin?"

"No, not like that. What she meant was… N-no, never mind! It's nothing!"

Her eyes suddenly went wide. For some reason, her face quickly turned red.

"I can't tell you, obviously!"

"Well, you almost did."

"It's personal! I—I mean… If I told you about it…"

"If you did?"

"I couldn't!"

"Which is it?!"

Iska was getting more and more confused. He realized it had been her sister who had bothered her, but he didn't understand why she was being so obstinate about not telling him anything else.

"What is it…? Huh?"

CHAPTER 5

He was receiving a call on his comm, but it wasn't from Jhin. It was Commander Mismis.

"Iska, it's an emergency!"

"What's wrong, Commander?"

"They say Ms. Alice is going on a rampage in the central base!"

"Excuse me?"

He doubted his own ears.

"It's the indoor training grounds at the central base! She's taken several soldiers hostage!"

"Wait, Commander."

"You need to go—hurry!"

"But I'm guarding her right now. She's right in front of me."

"Huh?"

He could practically hear Commander Mismis tilting her head quizzically over the comm.

"You're guarding her?"

"Yes. Actually, she's listening in right now."

When Iska looked at her from the corner of his eye, Alice was pointing at herself as if to say, *But I'm right here?*

"! Then it's someone else?!"

"Someone else? Why did you even think it was Alice in the first place…?"

"Because it was an emergency message from headquarters! That a witch they captured is going on a rampage. And she's supposed to be a purebred type, so I was convinced she had to be Ms. Alice…"

"It's not Alice. It has to be someone else."

But who?

If headquarters' information was to be believed, it was a purebred type they already had in their custody. But all the Zoa elite forces had been comatose…

"Wait, no!"

There was one person it could be. Among the Zoa, only one purebred type had escaped that fate.

"Commander!" he yelled into the comm. "I'll head there right away. Get all the other soldiers away from there!"

"What? I-is everything okay?!"

"You're right that she's a dangerous purebred type. Tanks and missiles won't work against her. The more you throw at her, the more casualties there'll be!"

It was the thorn astral mage, Kissing. She'd been transported with Lord Mask. If she used her powers, steel doors and barriers were as good as meaningless to her.

"And at a time like this…!"

With the comm still in his hand, Iska flipped around. For a moment, right before he'd turned away, he thought Alice had been looking at him as if she had something to say. He had felt that way, at least.

But he didn't have the time to check and ran out of the room.

Iska ran.

He had left her in the room alone. She took it as a message that he trusted her, considering she was a dangerous enemy and the Ice Calamity Witch.

"…"

She couldn't hear his footsteps anymore. Iska was surprisingly quiet to begin with. She remembered Rin having said something similar in the past, but now he was already so far away, she couldn't even sense his presence anymore.

CHAPTER 5

She was alone again. Alone in the room, Alice remembered what her sister had said.

"This is a story between a witch and a knight."
"This is the difference between the two of us. I have a knight by my side."

She leaned back against the wall and placed a hand on her breast. Then she gritted her teeth.

"I...could never...say that to him..." She spat out the words like she was throwing them away.

Just earlier, Alice simply hadn't been able to say the words. She couldn't tell him what her sister had said. That a witch needed a knight to protect her. It had happened the moment she'd seen Iska's face. A future that could be had come to her mind.

......What if I had told him I wanted to fight, too?
......What if I'd asked him to be my knight?

It would have been a convenient plea. Maybe Iska could fight alongside her. She'd started to feel like it could happen, and that was also why she couldn't tell him.

They had only one relationship with each other. The moment she wished for Iska to be a fully united front with her, everything would likely change.

The relationship between a witch and a knight.
When that happens...

...we'll no longer be rivals.

She was frightened of that.

With Iska in front of her, she was afraid of her comfortable connection with him crumbling.

"..." She set her chin on her knees.

"It's not like I could say that...," Alice murmured in a voice that seemed close to fading away.

4

The evening wind was becoming stronger and harsher. He'd arrived late at night at the central base. What had initially been a soft breeze that caressed the blades of grass had turned into a tempest that made the trees bow over.

"Is this it?!"

The sun had sunk.

As dark clouds covered the sky, he came across a two-story building that was aglow with lights.

"Huh?!"

The Imperial forces' indoor maneuvering grounds. Iska gulped when he saw the gate to the grounds had disappeared without a trace. The door and lock, the surveillance cameras, and even the surrounding walls had disappeared as though a giant eraser had been taken to them. The physical matter had been erased through the Thorn astral power.

The atrocious destruction reminded him what a threat purebred types really were. Faced with this astral power, the Imperial forces' fortifications were almost meaningless.

......*When I fought her before, I was out in the wild at a canyon.*

......*I understood this before, but when astral power goes on a rampage, everything's over in a city!*

Maneuvering grounds.

A field that mimicked the vast wastelands spread out before him. The gray sand and hard bedrock created steep slopes. Several

CHAPTER 5

large boulders were piled so tall that Iska had to crane his neck to look up at them as they formed something like a mountain range.

"I was growing tired of waiting," he heard a charming voice say to him.

When Iska turned around, he found a gigantic hole in the grounds' roof, revealing part of the night sky.

And there stood a girl with the moon shining behind her.

"I am Kissing Zoa Nebulis IX."

The black-haired girl turned around. She wore no blindfold. Her eyes, where her astral crest was, were slightly glittering.

"You may call me Kissing."

"I know that."

"We are not on equal terms yet."

"……?"

They stared at each other silently for ten seconds before Iska finally realized that had been her way of asking for his identity.

"You want to know my name?"

"Please think of it as an honor. This will be the first time I remember anyone's name except my dear uncle's."

"……Iska."

"Well then, Iska."

The girl flung open her arms.

It was almost like an insect unfurling its wings. Above her head, a countless number of black thorns had appeared, blotting out the ceiling.

"Let us go to war."

CHAPTER 6

Even if the Moon Were to Crumble

The scene could nearly be described as fantastical. Under the pale moonlight, the black-haired girl seemed to float vaguely.

She seemed endearing and fragile.

However...from the many thorns surrounding her, Iska knew she secretly carried a heinous power that did not match her appearance.

"A war?"

"I'm an astral mage, and you're an Imperial soldier. When we meet, we fight, don't we?"

"..."

"But please rest assured." Kissing, the thorn purebred type, stared at him with her glimmering eyes. "I haven't hurt a single Imperial soldier while coming here. Though I have taken down some buildings."

"Huh?!"

He doubted his own ears. He hadn't expected a purebred type from the Sovereignty to ever say anything like that.

"Even if you're trying to throw me off, I'll figure out right away if that's true or not."

"I wouldn't lie. My uncle has taught me it isn't good to lie."

"Then why?"

"Because I'm only after you."

Was it for revenge? Because of their fight at Mudor to secure the vortex? Was she after Iska in retaliation?

......*No, that doesn't explain it.*

......*She wouldn't keep away from the other soldiers if her only goal was me.*

He didn't understand. The most troubling thing of all was how Kissing behaved. She wasn't like Alice or Rin. When the girl fought, she was practically emotionless. He couldn't read her.

"Then what's your goal...?"

"Ability release."

Thousands of thorns gathered in the air, and converged into one from which something appeared.

"Re-form."

"Huh?!"

It was her secret move.

She could re-create the last things she destroyed. At Mudor, she had re-created a short-distance Imperial forces missile and caused a large explosion.

"Did you disassemble something ahead of time?!"

Without any hesitation, Iska leaped back as far as he could. This was an Imperial base. All kinds of explosive components were stored here. If she'd stolen one of those ahead of time...

He watched for an explosion, for flames, but instead, what appeared in front of Iska's eyes rolled along the ground. They were fist-size objects designed to be lobbed, but they weren't bombs.

"Stun grenades?!"

She had gotten him.

Iska had been staring at them, expecting them to explode, but the moment he realized what they were, the ten re-created grenades all went off at once. He saw them flash.

CHAPTER 6

His eyes were flooded with white light at point-blank range.

He couldn't believe it—a powerful astral mage had resorted to a sneak attack in order to blind him.

"You can dodge fire and explosions, so I thought about it for a long time—I thought about what Uncle On would do in order to stop you."

"……Guh!"

He reevaluated his opinion of Kissing. She wasn't anything like Alice or the Founder. This girl was a purebred type who used Thorn—and she could strategize just like Lord Mask.

"Astral-power expansion."

The condensed thorns burst. Several thousand thorns split into ten thousand and filled the sky above the indoor maneuvering ground.

"Become 'Stars.'"

In the span of one second, the thorns in midair fell to the ground. It was like a meteor shower. Falling at perilous speeds, they pierced everything on the ground one after another. When the thorns hit a gigantic boulder, it was obliterated. And when they hit the walls, they became riddled with holes. They created craters in the ground.

She destroyed everything around them. However, only the astral swords that could cut through astral power itself couldn't be disintegrated by the thorns.

"Hah!"

Iska stepped forward toward the shower of thorns. He swiveled around on the spot. He dashed and weaved through the rain of thorns that fell at a diagonal, narrowly avoiding being hit. He couldn't stop even for a moment.

He sliced through the thorns falling in front of him in a single stroke.

Then he knocked away the ones coming at him from above in his blind spot without so much as looking at them.

"No…"

The black-haired girl backed away. She looked overwhelmed, as though she'd seen something unbelievable.

"You can still see?"

"I can finally see now."

"Huh?!"

"If I had seen these thorns from the beginning, they would have gotten me."

He had lost his vision because of the stun grenades, and it was only now coming back.

The countless thorns falling could be compared to being targeted by several machine guns. Kissing was the only one controlling them, however, so all he had to do was run. Since she was controlling the thorn "bullets," he simply ran faster than she could aim them.

That was why she always missed.

The moment Kissing aimed at Iska, he would already be farther ahead.

"Don't come near me!" Kissing's voice was stiff. She thrust both her hands in front of her and tried her hardest to squeeze out the words. "March of thorns—the Whole of Creation…"

"Stop."

"Ugh!"

She shuddered.

She felt something hard against her neck. Right before she could attack him again, he had leaped close enough to thrust his black sword at her, but there were still thorns floating in the air.

"Cease using your astral power."

"I have a question for you," Kissing said.

CHAPTER 6

"I get to make the demands here," he reminded her, but she asked him regardless.

"Can you win against Elletear?"

"...What did you just say?"

"I will surrender."

In front of Iska's eyes as he held his blade at her, the thorns revolving overhead gently fell to the ground. Instead of disappearing, they lined up once they fell.

"I wanted to test your abilities. I apologize for having been rude."

It was proof of her surrender. Like a soldier putting down their gun, she had laid down her weapons to show she wouldn't resist.

"Iska, I would like to offer you a trade."

The girl crouched down.

She was on her knees and bowed.

"Please fight the witch Elletear alongside me. I will give you all my thorns."

EPILOGUE

The Dream That You, the Lord, Saw

Yunmelngen had a dream.

This was the dream. And even though they knew it was a dream, they could not resist it, nor could they wake from the nightmare. And that was how they had realized it.

This dream was a prophecy that the astral powers were trying to show them.

They fell.

In the dream, Yunmelngen sank hundreds of meters, then thousands, into the planet, like they were sinking into the dark ocean's depths.

They fell through the roads, the crust, the rock bed, even the lava, passing right through everything, deep into the planet.

"**Crow?!**" they yelled out of fear. They were afraid of sinking deeper into the dark depths of the planet alone and reached out for the surface. "**Crow?! Help me! I'm here…!**"

They received no response. The man they trusted most did not come running to save them.

Of course he couldn't. This was a dream the astral powers were showing them. And so all they could do was sink deeper alone into the planet as the astral powers wished.

"Ugh."

Suddenly, there was light.

Yunmelngen looked below; deep in the planet, they saw red, blue, green, white, yellow, purple, and countless other lights glittering and rising.

It was a vortex. It had been created from the planet's core—astral energy rising from the depths.

It was a great migration of astral powers. But why were the powers moving to the surface like this?

"They're running... The Eight Great Apostles. You must have known that, too..."

The astral powers were afraid. They had fled from their home, the planet's core, all the way to the surface. That was what the vortex actually was.

Once astral powers left the planet's core, they couldn't continue existing in their pure form, so they would erupt through a vortex and take possession of a human on the surface.

In which case...

What were the astral powers running from?

"The astral powers... You all were probably trying to show me this..."

The astral power in *them* was attempting to show them this. The power in Lord Yunmelngen was called the Planet's Defense,

EPILOGUE

and so Yunmelngen would be the most sensitive to dangers threatening the planet.

Therefore, the powers were warning Yunmelngen.

Yunmelngen continued to sink deeper, and as they reached the abyss that was the planet's core, they realized something was there that shouldn't have been.

"That's it!"

There it was.

They were at the planet's abyss. The scorching heat of the lava acted as the thing's cradle.

And the abomination that was like astral power but also not, stirred and seemed to pulsate.

It writhed like an exposed heart. In the heat of the lava that could have melted steel, it slept quietly and grew. This was the calamity that the Astrals feared and called the Planet's Demise.

In other words, it was the World Enemy.

And its name was…

"La Selah Milah Uls…"

Yunmelngen did not know where the name came from and did not intend to find out.

But what was most abominable of all…

This calamity transformed humans and astral power into grotesque monsters, into enemies.

One human had become the fallen angel Kelvina.

Another the witch Vichyssoise.

And another the witch Elletear.

Astral power into an eidos of the earth.

And into an eidos of the sea.

All would be corrupted into an abomination.

And the astral powers, in fear of that, had fled the planet's core.

"So you're the cause of this…"

As Yunmelngen glared at the abomination writhing deep within the abyss, they bared their teeth.

If only the calamity had never existed…

There never would have been a vortex. The astral powers would have never fled. Astral power could have remained astral power. And humans could have remained human.

"…Tsk!"

Then they felt a sharp pain in their chest. Though they were in a dream, the pain felt real.

That was right.

They were also possessed by this power, and that was why they had transformed into this.

No astral power or astral mage could win against the calamity.

"I know that…"

As they clutched their chest, they glared down at the calamity.

"You don't even see me as an enemy…"

The monster probably didn't even notice Yunmelngen was having this dream. Even though it created such fear and nightmares for others, the monster itself was soundly asleep.

In that case…

"You can just stay asleep."

And this was what they had to say to it, to the disaster that sought to desecrate both astral powers and humanity: **"While**

EPILOGUE

you've been here gathering strength for decades or centuries, humans will keep giving birth to new generations… No, they already have, and they've continued to change!"

Yunmelngen believed they would be able to find it. They swore they would. In these hundred years.

"Even if I can't defeat you myself…!"

It would not be the Founder Nebulis or Crossweil the Black Steel Gladiator.

The only one who could fight against the calamity was the successor and his astral swords.

And…those who wished to help him.

"You'll see! We'll go for your throat, World Enemy!"

"Lor—"

"Lord? Lord?"

They felt something brush their shoulders. Yunmelngen realized only after opening their eyes slightly that someone was jostling them.

"Um, you were making a very scary face…"

The girl with strawberry-blond hair was looking at them in fear. It seemed she had been watching them as they slept.

"What is it, Princess Sisbell? Didn't I say I would sleep?"

"B-but your face was so frightening that I thought something was wrong! You were gritting your teeth and groaning!"

"Hmm…"

They had seen that dream, after all. Of course they would look rather frightening in their sleep, given that.

"Well, it's all right, then… Hmm."

They stretched and enthusiastically got up. Surprisingly, they weren't drowsy. They couldn't tell if it was because they had been woken or because they were free of the nightmare.

"All right, I'm awake. Princess Sisbell, please bring over your sister. And that amusing attendant."

"Do you mean my sister Alice and Rin?"

"Oh yes, and the four from Unit 907."

"Out of curiosity, why do you need them?"

"To talk about a dream."

When the princess gave them a strange look, Yunmelngen bit back a yawn.

"I'll tell everyone about the dream I saw. And about the cause of all this."

Afterword

"Well then, Iska, let us go to war."

Thank you for picking up the twelfth volume of *Our Last Crusade or the Rise of a New World*!

First, I am terribly sorry for the wait.

I had a certain happy announcement (mentioned later) that I wanted to make along with the publication of this book, so the pace was a little slower than usual. I feel like this twelfth volume was a proper follow-up to the eleventh.

The power dynamics are really at play in the Empire and Sovereignty.

I think the biggest change was in the Zoa princess.

Although she first appeared in the second volume as a powerful purebred type, I hadn't been able to write about her much until now.

And it was the first time she'd said anyone's name except Lord Mask's…

AFTERWORD

I think you can look forward to seeing how she grows.

As for Alice, she faced her older sister, and we'll get to see how she takes her sister's words. The continuation will be very exciting, so I hope you look forward to it!

Now, then…

That's enough for this volume. I have one announcement to make this time.

And it's a very happy one.

The *Last Crusade* anime is getting a sequel!

Before you read this afterword, it would have already been announced on October 1 on the official website and other social media.

I'm writing this in September, so I can only imagine the mood after the announcement, but I think many people will be surprised by it!

Now that I think about it, the first season of the anime aired just a year ago.

Of course, I didn't know whether the anime would continue before it was broadcast, but apparently because many people supported it, the anime is getting a sequel.

I was very surprised when I heard about it!

To everyone who watched the anime, tweeted about their impressions, bought the Blu-ray, DVDs, or commemorative merch, and most of all to you, the fans who have supported the novels, I would like to take this opportunity to say you have my gratitude.

Thank you very, very much!

※Like the first season, announcements will be made on the *Last Crusade* official Twitter (https://twitter.com/kimisen_project). I hope you'll take this opportunity to follow it!

AFTERWORD

* * *

Now then, that's enough for *Last Crusade*.

I'd like to make an announcement about another series.

While *Last Crusade* is going swimmingly, as usual, with the anime announcement, there's one other story I'd like your support on!

▼MF Bunko J *Gods' Games We Play* Volume 3 is on sale!

A fantasy battle of the wits of humanity vs. the gods.

Humanity must win ten games of wits against the gods to achieve victory. In the history of mankind, no one has yet to clear them all. In this tale, a young man takes up the impossible challenge.

According to reader votes for the Light Novel News Online Award, the second volume had a favorable response, so I'm happy to say that it's getting a manga adaptation in *Gekkan Comic Alive*!

Since it just started at the beginning of the year, I would be so happy if you supported it along with *Last Crusade*!

And so, the afterword has come to an end.

To everyone who has been so kind to me, to Ao Nekonabe, it finally happened! Thank you for the much-awaited, beautiful cover illustration of the Founder Nebulis!

Actually, Iska and Alice's first battle together was against her now that I think about it.

A huge boss like her is finally on the cover… It really makes me feel like we finally reached the second half of this story. Joheim's and Elletear's new designs were also superb and wonderful!

The anime sequel is coming, so I hope you'll continue to follow along!

To my editors O and S, it has been so reassuring to have you in charge of my novels, of course, and now for the anime sequel. I

AFTERWORD

hope to make *Last Crusade* even bigger and more exciting than last year, so I hope for your assistance in the future as well!

Well, then…

Normally I finish thanking everyone here, but this time I have one more group to thank.

To those who worked on the first season of the anime, that was the first time my work got an anime adaptation. I was so happy, and it was an honor to have a top-notch production, so I am eternally grateful.

Once again, thank you very much!

Well then, here's the final announcement.

Next is *Last Crusade* Volume 13.

A tale of the swordsman Iska and the witch princess Alice.

Alice had resolved to stay in the Empire.

And Iska is her guard. The curtain opens on their new life in the capital, where they've begun to become even more conscious of each other.

While Lord Yunmelngen shares a secret that gives them a sense of the approaching war.

And when the two head to the forbidden land that's neither in the Empire nor the Sovereignty, they see…

Winter 2022: MF Bunko J, *Gods' Games We Play* Volume 4.

Winter 2022: *Last Crusade* Volume 13.

I hope we'll meet each other again then!

The story will continue full speed ahead in the next volume, so I hope you look forward to it!

Between summer and fall,

Kei Sazane

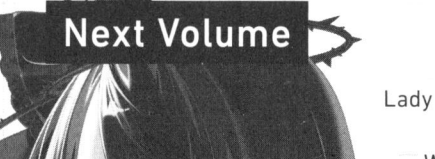

Lady Alice? Where is Lady Alice? What?! She went outside with the Imperial swordsman?

All in order to defeat Elletear, the Zoa princess approaches Iska to form an allegiance. Meanwhile, Alice is still shaken by her sister's words and receives an order from the Lord.

She is told to go to the forbidden land that is neither part of the Empire nor the Sovereignty.

The thirteenth act of the Supreme Witch and the most powerful swordsman's dance.

Iska, have you ever thought about becoming someone's knight?

Our Last CRUSADE OR THE RISE OF A New World

VOLUME 13
Coming summer of 2024!